Last Retailer Standing

Relevant Leadership Relevant Brand

By George Minakakis

First Edition – March 2013

Canadian Edition
Last Retailer Standing
Relevant Leadership Relevant Brand

ISBN
978-0-9918-8080-5 (Paperback)

Produced by:

FriesenPress
Suite 300 – 852 Fort Street
Victoria, BC, Canada V8W 1H8

www.friesenpress.com

Table of Contents

To my wife, children and little Cruz
for your inspiration, trust, and love.

And to Mom & Dad
for teaching me to ask, "what if?"

For more information on George Minakakis visit

www.georgeminakakis.com

Prologue

AT THE END OF THIS book you will understand one key lesson that is as unforgiving as pursuing the wrong strategies. The lesson is that if the leadership of the brand is not relevant the brand itself will not be relevant.

It is without question that business in general and society, have had to endure a great deal of challenges in the last four years. It is likely that we will have to endure this cycle for another four years until we purge many of the toxic decisions we've made in the past. Twenty-five years ago a new revolution began in business, it started with a 'service revolution' that came complete with Mission, Vision and Value statements. That was followed by organizations going through 'cultural revolutions' inspiring their devoted employees to be comfortable with change and to act as intrapreneurs in the business and a quasi freedom to act within their roles. The buzzwords of the time were 'outsourcing', 'just-in time', 'thinking outside the box', 'best practices' and 'metrics', just to name a few. And here we are in the 21st Century faced with not just globalization, but a looming fear that it could collapse because demand doesn't seem sustainable. And in all of this, twenty-five years later I contend that yesterday's leadership and management practices are no longer adequate to save the day. After all, we may be facing creative destruction which is the replacement of old redundant industries with new ones in which case changes the landscape for workers, consumers and investors. It is not that the world is coming to an end it is the beginning of a new one. The future will be about speed to market, staying relevant and social responsibility (personal and corporate), which means being transparent and accountable for your actions. Therefore, leaders and managers who are still holding on to past vested ideas about leadership and management will need to change themselves or be replaced, for an organization to remain relevant and competitive. We may be surprised about future leadership because they will not necessarily be the under 40 (youthful and a risk taker) or the over 60 (with years of business experience) they will simply be the leaders who understand how to be effective in today's world.

Introduction

For as long as I can remember, I have wanted to be in the retail industry for two reasons: first, the behaviour of consumers has always intrigued me, and secondly, the power of effective marketing to attract consumers with branding, product, and pricing strategies fascinates me.

I grew up in Montréal. Not far from our home was a corner convenience store called Johnny's. Every once in a while I was sent there on an important mission to buy a few things for my mother. My reward was a Pepsi or Coke, with no questions asked about my choice. Johnny ran a clean, organized store. Everything had its place and no shelf was ever empty. In the summer months the Coke bottles were chilling in the water-cooled refrigerator, while the candy and ice cream were abundant.

Just down the road, another store soon opened. It was bigger and had an expanded product assortment. The store had more lighting, new cash registers, and everyone was in uniform. I remember visiting that store on some of my missions as well, and it was always busy. After a while, Johnny's couldn't keep its shelves stocked anymore, so my mother asked me to go only to the other store. In about a year's time, Johnny's was gone. My father said the store had been there for years. As a kid I kind of understood why Johnny's shut its doors, but back then I wasn't sure what he could have done about it. This book is for all the retailers that don't want Johnny's business experience – that is, becoming competitively irrelevant.

The one thing that I know with certainty is that 70-80% of the retail businesses operating today will either fail or be acquired and converted into another brand within the next 10-20 years. So why bother putting a lot of effort into trying to change an industry that is easily overwhelmed by disruptive forces? Simply, the answer is that it does not have to be that way, especially if you can catch and prevent the mistakes that occur in other retail brands from occurring in yours. Equally important is to understand how to remain competitive and relevant; in this case you cannot achieve the first objective in the long term without the latter being a part of your culture. There is no escaping this, if you want the brand you lead or own to succeed, you must change the way you lead and operate your business.

The second challenge to this and other industries is the impact that technology will and is having on operators, employees and consumers alike. What used to be the norm is now being revolutionized in such manner that technology is now a disruptive competitive force. Further, no government, brand, or institution can ignore the role of technology and how the speed with which people are making choices is reshaping how we shop, live, and communicate with one another. And as a retailer whether you are an independent, chain, or conglomerate you need to understand this shift is being driven by your customers and disruptive competitors.

The third challenge is a broader discussion and a question of leadership – it takes a lot of courage to say no to a direction that you know will negatively impact service, sales, and market share and yet everyday countless executives continue to make the same mistakes. Retailers whose businesses are failing to meet their objectives, could have a different outcome if they found better solutions than reducing service hours, dismantling their internal business cultures, slashing their marketing budgets, and just offering more discounts. There is a shortfall in strategic thinking when businesses reach this stage of their end game and as a result employee's, customers and shareholders want someone to be accountable.

These challenges are significant and few will likely survive them in the long-term, especially once the downward spiral begins it becomes more difficult to rebound. The most urgent goal a leadership team of any retail company can embrace is to remain relevant in a competitive and changing marketplace.

While writing this book I also asked myself, what do I dislike about business books as an executive? The answer was simple: it takes too long to get to the point. I have written this book for executives and operators who want to get to the core of the issues they face and review their options fast. All the chapters are brief and to the point, and include guiding principles at the beginning and executive notes at the end. I don't claim that my approach to running a retail business will guarantee every retailer success. However, I hope that after 20 years of leading retail brands domestically and internationally, my insights will help you determine your next strategic choices in this interesting era in which everyone needs to remain relevant and competitive.

It doesn't matter if you are in retail, the airline industry, own a medical practice, operate a restaurant franchise or run a law practice, many of the principles and key learnings in this book apply to just about every industry. Success is not a matter of luck. We live in an era where financial markets don't get excited unless you are cutting costs or closing plants, at least that's how it appears. The truth is the market is looking for signs that you are able to stay relevant with consumers and the end users of your services. If you are relevant you are growing sales and profits, if you are not relevant you are losing market share, customers and missing important changes in your industry. So this book applies to everyone and to many industries, I chose retail because it has been my business world for over 20 years.

At the beginning of this introduction I referenced to relevant leaders equating to the making of relevant brands. Symbolically leaders are the reason why brands succeed or fail. I also don't want to give you the impression that you have to hire someone from your industry to be successful. Although many publicly traded companies try to bring in a leader with a reputation, and the intent is usually to appease the markets and hope for better share price. History of course has shown us that this isn't always the outcome. What you will learn in this book is that there are solutions to improving your performance and that fundamentally in the spirit of sound leadership and management you can evolve and survive in difficult and opportune times.

Chapter Summary and Overview

THE SUMMARY THAT FOLLOWS PROVIDES some context on how each of these chapters is connected in building a foundation for retailers that want to review the challenges and address the opportunities.

Chapter 1: The Current Retail Industry

The retail sector has been challenged by many economic, competitive, technological and social changes over the last five years. Each retailer in this sector is about to face some serious challenges on how to remain relevant in the market place. This chapter selectively points out many of the obstacles that need to be considered and addressed.

Chapter 2: Longevity

One of the biggest challenges companies face today is being able to stay in the game as a viable business. And the remarkable thing is that many have discovered that there is an important alchemy to this equation. It is not a mystery or information left to a few plutocrats in the industry, we have all been taught its importance in business schools and during our careers. Even though we understand it to be culture we fail to leverage its importance and how to make it more effective.

Chapter 3: Evolve or Perish

There is no doubt that companies will continue to fail and the real lesson comes down to how well a strategy can defend against competitors and prevent customers from migrating to trial other retailers. At the heart of strategy is the organization and its culture, can it and will it be able to address the issues ahead?

Chapter 4: The Global Retail Challenges

There is an advantage to have traveled and been schooled about the retail industry at a global level such as I have. You are not mitigated by old school or cultural boundaries that stymy so many retailers from long-term growth. However, what is interesting aside from cultural differences the dynamics of competing do not differ that much with the exception of regulated and protected markets.

Chapter 5: Why Retailers Fail – One Retailer's Tale

This chapter is an attempt to show how the calamity of everything I have described can and does happen in real life. The story isn't true, yet many who have read it, nod their heads with points that they have personally experienced.

Chapter 6: Pursuing the Wrong Strategies

Is the strategy viable, deliverable, can you rally employees and customers to get excited by it? Or is it an internal initiative that really doesn't address how to win and merely the notion that you might win. I once attended a marketing seminar and heard a marketer talk about how they were going to train customers. It seems to me that customers have been training us, sale after sale after sale event.

Chapter 7 & 8: The Dilemma of Online versus Offline (Part One and Two)

As you progress through the book I want you to realize that ignoring the online world will only have a negative outcome. If your brand isn't growing their online revenue and asking the tough questions about your offline business, your brand does not understand the importance of being relevant to create longevity.

Chapter 9: Customer Conversion – the Myths and Reality

This is one of my favourite chapters. People sell the products and services these don't sell themselves and unless a retailer understands how to create that environment in their stores they will miss the biggest opportunity to grow their business. I have seen just about every conceivable idea imagined to grow customer conversion and transactions, yet it all comes down to one thing. Your people need to be advocates or it just will not happen.

Chapter 10: The Right Consumer Model

How is your consumer model performing? Can you drive growth and sustain your position in the market or is it time for change? I define four categories that retailer's fall under, and you need to decide for yourself where you belong, before you begin to develop strategies to keep yourself relevant.

Chapter 11: When is Change Needed?

Once you have defined how your brand is positioned you can begin thinking on whether it is time for change. And if it is, the task ahead will require strong leadership and careful assessment.

Chapter 12: Leadership

Just as the sub-titles suggest, the leadership of the organization needs to be relevant for the brand to do the same. I review the operational and executive leadership styles that work and don't work in a retail environment. This sets the stage for understanding your true organizational effectiveness.

Chapter 13: A Stress Test for Retailers

Retailers sometimes can get so locked into their own 'mental process' that they fail to see the external environment for what it is. I developed a simple model to test your ability to compete however and arguably, you may need to adjust the parameters of your own test. Ultimately the question is, do you have the ability to change, compete and stay relevant? It all begins with being honest.

Chapter 14: Competitive Endurance

Spinning off from the stress test this chapter sets the stage for guiding your brand to become relevant. I question an organization's internal competencies and capabilities to pursue and develop strategies that will sustain a brand's longevity in the market place.

Chapter 15: How Successful Retail Brands Win

The subtitle of this chapter describes the content best, your end goal is to 'stay in the game'. There are four quadrants that define where your brand may fit-in. Once again it is about being tough on yourself versus your competencies and capabilities. Are you achieving your goals in the market and can you sustain them?

Chapter 16: The "S Factor"

To be clear the letter 'S' stands for service and you could argue it also stands for strategy, yet they are intertwined. In my personal experience I define what works as a formula to achieve a higher level of sustainable customer experience. It's not price that grows a business, price is only a determinant for what a consumer is willing to pay for, what you have to offer and the way your value proposition delivers it. Get those two right and you have a winning formula.

Chapter 17: Beyond the Financials

I have a very strong perspective that people who just read the top and bottom line numbers and take what they are being told at face value for the gains and shortfalls are setting themselves up for disappointment. People generate results, sales and profits; simply ask a lot of questions about how they did it and what's missing. You will be pleasantly surprised to learn what is working and what isn't.

Chapter 18: Governance and Organizational Responsibility

No executive at any level should dismiss the importance of corporate social responsibility, it needs to be woven into all for and not for profit organizations. Above all it needs to be more than just statements the organizations, consumers and stakeholders have to see it and believe it.

Chapter 19: Where Was the Board?

This is a brief chapter on corporate governance and it is only an outline on how boards sometimes miss their duty to address opportunities and threats.

Chapter 20: Competitive Advantage of Employee Engagement

Look at organizations with low turnover, high on employee development with true succession planning and you will find an organization that can deliver results.

All of this boils down to a leadership question. Are employees an asset that appreciates or a cost?

Chapter 21: Personal Social Responsibility – Cultural Divides

I could have written another book on this subject because it speaks to the importance of responsible leadership. The next generation of leaders, in the not too distant future will have a greater balancing act to deliver within a company, as a board director and socially with the public. Your reputation will be everything.

Chapter 22: Last Retailer Standing

Simply it would be naïve of me to say that there will only be one winner in the market place. However, there is always only one leader in each segment of the retail industry. The chapter is also followed with a closing statement on leadership, it is the reason why organizations succeed or fail, hence relevant leadership, relevant brand.

Summary of Principles:

At the end of this book there is also a summary of all the principles defined throughout the text.

Priority I: Cause and Effect - Know Where It Started

THE CHINESE REFER TO THE Iron Rice Bowl as a means to define their preoccupation with a job for life or security of their wealth. The saying translated goes like this.

"If you do nothing you risk nothing, if you do a little you risk a little, if you do a lot you risk a lot."

The saying above also depicts how a risk adverse business leader and culture can find itself in trouble. Businesses in every industry, culture and country find themselves facing change and yet they become paralyzed by one or two bad decisions. It is from that lesson and experience that they begin to play it safe therefore doing nothing, or a little of something that is ineffective or too much of the same and making no difference in outcome.

The potential for failure in the retail industry is generally high. If the banks and investors don't give up on your business, either the consumers or your employees will – sometimes all of them at the same time. Some retailers are lucky and rebound. Others sell to a chain, and yet others close out. The reasons for failure are always the same: someone in management did not recognize the need for change and the pursuit of opportunity.

In my opinion, the important factors toward longevity are the capabilities related to being competitive and relevant. No business will survive in an industry where fashion, services, and products continue to evolve without taking these factors into account. And the wrong choices in any of these areas can be extremely unforgiving in the cycle of a brand.

It does not matter if you are the chairperson, board director, chief executive officer, chief operating officer, president of a division, vice-president of operations for a region, a field manager, or a store manager – your decisions and effectiveness impact the outcomes of the retail organization you work for and lead. Whether you sell shoes, car mufflers, garden tools, lumber, groceries, clothing, or jewellery, your business is going to face more competition during the next five years than ever before. Your strategies will become weaker, and old promotional offers that you used to rely on will become less interesting to a very interconnected society. At the end of the day, leaders have a personal social responsibility to the employees, customers, and shareholders of these retail companies to ensure their long-term success.

In conjunction to this, the choices founders and boards make in leaders and business strategies will change the course of the company, however not always favourably or with the outcomes expected.

Chapter 1: The Current Retail Industry

Principle 1: Change is imminent.

Sales performance is everything in the world of merchants, yet it all comes down to the effectiveness of an organization's strategies to win and retain loyal customers. Business analysts follow the retail industry closely, and for obvious reasons – how consumers choose to spend their money will determine how retailers in all categories perform financially. And don't forget that this is also a barometer for economists, as the service industry is a significant contributor to GDP.

Of course, some retailers struggle with the growth of online competitors and the danger of remaining offline, sticking only with brick and mortar stores. It should not come as a surprise that this shift is occurring in an industry that is experiencing only marginal growth. The online models are breaking away and delivering higher comparable sales increases.

Online retailing is at the top of all retail executives' agendas. The main issues are how to make it effective and what impact it will have on their bricks and mortar (offline) business. In addition, the entry of new competitors with fresh models and their ability to draw sales from existing retailers is a risk that doesn't get addressed as effectively as it could be.

We are on the cusp of two major changes: how retailers will sell to consumers, and how consumers will in turn choose to buy. The two may not be aligned, considering the struggles with growth that many retailers are encountering. And for that matter, service has changed – or rather, the industry itself has changed how much service consumers receive.

Consider iPad's incredible sales and how people are inundating social networks. If there were no ecosystem of humans with the need for this level of technology, it would not exist as pervasively as it does today. As a result, change in the retail category is no longer just looming, it is being formulated and developed for the same reason–need. The need in this case is that consumers are looking for a more personal and interactive relationship with retailers. On the other hand, when you visit many retail stores, service is something that is hard to come by. In fact, many retailers have unwittingly created a self-serve environment.

While watching TV one day, I heard the announcer for a commercial about online dating state that today, 1 in 5 couples meet with the assistance of online dating platforms. If it is true that 20% of the North American population is actually comfortable using technology for personal relationships (online dating), then technology has been elevated to a high level of trust. Further proof lies in how we have embraced social networks with millions of subscribers, such as Facebook (900 million), LinkedIn (150 million) and Twitter (500 million), to communicate, document our lives and experiences, share opinions and ideas, build consensus, and find opportunities. For those retailers who still dismiss online retailing as a major component of their future sales growth, perhaps this will help: Paypal's online activity was up by 26% in their most recent quarter. eBay's revenue for the same quarter was up by 29%, thanks to Paypal.

Nevertheless, retailers are still struggling with how to embrace social media and make it work for them. General Motors recently pulled back on their advertising with Facebook. When asked, some marketing departments tell you they're still working their online and social media strategies. My own analysis of social media is that if you are not getting a lift in awareness and sales from them, there are likely two reasons: your brand may not be relevant to consumers who are using social media, or your marketing department may not have the right capabilities and competencies on its team.

There are commonalities in the financial failures that retail brands experience. While some are recoverable, it all depends on the speed with which you react to the issues or challenges your business faces. Managing the short – and long-term performance of a retail brand has taken its toll on many. This is compounded by the uncertainties of a global economy, competition, and consumers shifting their shopping preferences. Brands also go through a cycle of relevance (that is, being relevant to a specific group of consumers) and irrelevance (when the culture and DNA of their business model is outdated). Unless retailers are prepared to reinvent themselves faster, the consequences can be economically irreversible. The most common first signs that it is too late to act is declining traffic and sales.

Retailers everywhere are searching for new tactics to influence consumers to buy from them. Of equal importance is to have consumers buy more, and more frequently. We all know that for every full percentage point of decline in sales, retailers respond with more sales events and excessive discounting. This ultimately erodes profit and the ability to stay in business. As a result, retailers inadvertently reduce their services. In the end, their overall customer experience not only diminishes, but their ability to retain talent and grow customer count are reduced, and eventually they lose consumers' interest.

Although business organizations around the world may have cleaned up their balance sheets and tightened up their cost structures, what is still missing is their ability grow their business and sustain that growth. We can argue that it is the fault of the economy, however the economy doesn't prevent you as a leader from being more competitive and expanding your business by pursuing your competitors' customers. At the core of this objective is your ability to remain relevant, sustain sales and service competencies in your operations, and deliver on your service promise.

At the heart of a sustainable business model is the strength of the leadership team's ability to define the right strategies, as well as manage a high level of implementation and execution. Management at times confuse the success of their business with the effectiveness of their administrative functions, strong reporting, and achievement of short-term sales objectives. A well-run company at the functional level is certainly an important aspect of maintaining order to achieve success. However, strategy in the retail world can never be fixated or immovable. One major reason that encompasses all issues is that so-called 'competitive forces' are arriving and evolving at a faster pace than in the past. I doubt that organizations conduct enough collective diligence to understand the markets they serve, the consumers they want to reach, and the manner in which they want to achieve their goals.

Competitive forces are everywhere in the retail industry, from disruptive new online consumer models, the entry of new retailers, changes in supply chain, and evolving demographics. With the speed of technological innovation, changes occur that are not always expected. I always ask, are we following or leading change? It is so easy to fall into a trap and think that we can capture some part of a trend. However, in an economy that is transitionally shifting to one with greater speed, innovation, and service, it will be harder for many retailers to keep up. We are also witnessing brands that create trends and lead within a category, while others continue to struggle with day-to-day operations.

Apple, for example, is a retailer's dream; they have high traffic, consumer demand, and the anticipation of loyal customers who are waiting for their next innovations. Are there more Apples out there? Perhaps. However, few have nailed down the complete model in this manner. Being successful over the next decade will require clear strategies to reach the right consumers with a local and national presence.

I do not believe that the majority of retailers are maximizing their full sales potential. Corporate boards need to be more active and respond with speed and decisiveness when a brand is struggling. A company that wishes to compete at a world class level should be creating trends, distinguishing themselves in service, demonstrating visible innovation, and becoming disrupters in a manner that retains and attracts new customers. There is also an opportunity for greater employee engagement. Being a socially responsible retailer not only creates the right framework for a sustainable culture, it also develops stronger relationships with customers and stakeholders. Why are more retailers not pursuing these strategies?

Why Retailers are not Maximizing Sales

To begin with, many retailers are not as operationally focused as they believe they are. Their service has eroded to a level where they are unable to meet and serve customers effectively. Competitively many have become inert and are unable to lead in their own category and management does not have enough focus on product, implementation and execution of strategies, and store level awareness of what is working and what does not work. In effect those that fail have removed themselves from what customers are looking for. The second issue is one of cost controls and this is not to suggest for a moment that it is not an important part of staying in business. However, some are so focused on managing costs that the leadership of the organization doesn't realize that they have polarized their organization on what's more important. The outcome in many instances is a continued decline in sales performance and in most cases management at the store level has no other focus. Of course the home office has sales goals by market, region and store nevertheless you can only serve one objective very well and it is usually the one that gives operations the least grief.

Underperforming Boards

There are boards that remain operationally distant from management. While in many cases this is their role, some boards have not been either properly advised or consulted by management, leading to the wrong strategies being pursued. Information is a vital element for a board to make informed decisions and it is possible the directors on boards that preside over retail companies may not have the right skills, or enough understanding of the business to challenge management to be more transparent in their execution of strategy. Of course in the last decade there have been plenty of failed companies where it appears that the boards have not effectively acted on their fiduciary duties. Boards have fundamentally three roles the first to ensure that the management team is pursuing the right strategies. The second to ensure that the financial performance and reporting of the company meets expectations and that there are no surprises in either. Their third responsibility is to place an emphasis on proper corporate governance, which in effect means fulfilling their duties as directors. Unfortunately, due to the part-time presence and involvement of boards something can go wrong in a fiscal quarter or was missed in past meetings. Essentially, retail companies fail because someone wasn't paying enough attention to the details.

Missing the Opportunities

Retailers that do not look for or create trends have become victims of others that do innovate. Online revenue growth is not a major focus for them. They do not bring enough technology to the store level to wow their customers. They rely on what used to work and are unable to reset their organization in the right direction to pursue and create opportunities for growth. I believe that history will show that many opportunities have always been discussed by organizations however the vision to pursue them was not adequate and perhaps dismissed. It is natural for leadership to assume that an idea or innovative market move may be premature or not a fit for a company to pursue. It also makes sense not to distract the business from its current focus, albeit there is no doubt that by the time an organization realizes that the need for change is critical it can also be too late.

Engaged Employees

No retailer or any other organization will succeed today without the internal population of workers being aligned. In the past, retail management may have believed that they were in control of their workforce because they hired them. However, today retailers need to understand that employees choose to work for them. And those choices are driven by cultural practices that align with the worker's desires to offer their services to an organization with an acceptable set of values.

Socially Responsible Organizations

The day of a more powerful employee, consumer and shareholder advocacy has arrived. This change in social behaviour will take its toll on less committed organizations that have dysfunctional business cultures and even less effective strategic capabilities. The failure of these organizations, and not just in retail, will be on the rise and expedited with the exodus of talent, buyers and investors. Management and boards need to see this as an important social shift and that a few mistakes can quickly derail what were once good intentions.

Executive Notes: A Lack of Knowledge or Execution

Retail organizations face many challenges and sometimes the root of issues related to sales and profit are easily clouded by misinformation, poor alignment and the pursuit of the wrong strategies.

- Not all stores are posting positive comparable sales.
- Product and pricing are not attractive to consumers.
- High employee turnover is driven by a loss in corporate culture.
- Change strategies have a negative impact on the brand's service culture.
- Training and development fail to deliver sales results, and each new initiative looks like the book-of-the-month club.
- Customer retention is slipping, and marketing has theories but no solutions.
- Rate of new customer growth is not keeping up with the needs of the business.
- E-commerce models are not interactive and are not engaging customers.
- Social media is not a competency within the organization, and it is a missed opportunity.
- Short-term push for sales results is overused and undermines the brand's image.
- Reinvestment in building brand equity is inadequate or ineffective.
- In-store procedures and best practices, if they exist, are not adhered to.
- The old marketing strategies keep being replayed in hopes of a different outcome.

- Corporate boards are inactive and response is slow and indecisive when a brand is struggling.

Chapter 2: Longevity

PRINCIPLE 2: PROTECT YOUR ORGANIZATIONAL culture and build its DNA in a direction that sustains a successful business model for the long-term.

The Oldest Companies in the World

The majority of new businesses fail within their first 12 to 18 months of operation. If they make it to five years it's because they have a competitive advantage or are selling to an underserved sector of the market. Once past the five year mark, if they are unable to evolve and expand, it's likely that they will not be around to see their tenth year. In this new economy where workers and consumers are more connected than ever before, sharing ideas and points of view can add or take away years from the future of a business.

Have you ever wondered why some businesses last longer than others, and why some retail brands don't last as long as expected? The answers are as complex as each business itself. To start with, what are the oldest businesses in the world, and why have they lasted as long as they have?

According to Wikipedia, the oldest company in the world is Nisiyama Onsen Kieunkan, a Japanese hotel founded in 705 AD. It claims to have had 52 operators in its 1307-year history. The oldest restaurant in the world is in Austria, called Stiftskeller St. Peter. It was founded in 803 AD. The restaurant resides within the monastery walls of St. Peter's Archabbey, Salzburg. This restaurant has a unique customer ecosystem of its own; since it resides in the confines of the abbey, its customer base is generally Christian. The oldest companies in the world are primarily from Japan and Northern Europe. If you were to read the history of these companies, you would find that many have experienced little change in tradition, culture, or values.

Unofficially, the oldest retailer in the world was founded in 1585, operating under the name of Mercros in Japan. Officially, the oldest retailers are both department stores. The oldest is Matsuzakaya, founded in 1611 in Japan. The oldest retailer in North America is the Hudson's Bay Trading company, founded on May 2, 1670 of course The Bay is no longer owned by Canadians.

How does a business last that long? And what takes place inside the culture of an organization of a successful business? When reading background information about these long-lasting businesses, it occurred to me that this longevity could be replicated by others by focussing on an important factor: culture. In fact, modern corporate businesses and business educators have been speaking about the importance of culture for the last fifty years. The definition of corporate culture in my opinion has never been well defined at the company level other than being formed by a few words on a mission or vision statement and in many cases the definition of culture evolves on its own. The principles and values needed, for a brand to succeed must be prescribed by the leadership and founders of the organization. What is generally missing is clarity on the inherent competency and capabilities of the organization and how they will be embraced to ensure that the brand lives up to its expectations. Such as; the ability to deliver innovative products and services, the capacity to identify how and why consumer preferences are shifting and what to do about it and the competencies behind delivering strategic initiatives with strong execution. And execution as a capability in itself is something that is also a struggle for many. Financially successful businesses start declining once culture begins to lose its momentum. Culture it seems is not something that a single business leader can manage alone it must have employees, customers, and other stakeholders who believe in the brand for one reason or another.

Many older businesses have been protected intentionally or unintentionally by culture. The hotel in Japan has been protected from the spoils of external cultures, passing through 52 owners for over 1,200 years with very little non-Japanese influence until the 1860s. Those who owned and operated the hotel knew enough to maintain key attributes important to the traditional culture. Similarly, the Austrian restaurant functions in an eco-culture, keeping its traditions and values in check through protection from the monks.

The Importance of Culture and Leadership

So what drives business longevity? The key factor is culture. The right culture is an important aspect of longevity, yet most companies are not able to sustain their internal cultures. What happens to culture is more a question of leadership rather than just applying the wrong strategies that prevent it from succeeding, although the strategies used are a substantial and contributing factor. With each leadership change that does not take into account the importance of an organization's legacy, a brand can and will lose its way.

The right leadership is also an important driver that sustains the future of a company. It takes a great deal of effort to find the right individual to be CEO of a company. However, executive search firms, like most companies, focus only on recruiting for executives with specific skills and experiences. What doesn't get included in the search are cultural fit and the ability to effectively manage major change initiatives. By not including these elements when searching for the right CEO, companies find themselves in peril. Some will fail or end up with a diluted position in the market place.

Company Lifespan is Decreasing

According to a study conducted by Ellen de Rooij of the Stratix Group, the average life expectancy of most companies is 12.5 years, including its start-up phase and peaks. By 2020, the average lifespan of a company in the S&P will have declined by 75%. According to Professor Richard Foster from Yale University, the average S&P 500 companies will have a lifespan of 15 years, versus 67 years in the 1920s. And a McKinsey study of the 74 companies that have stayed in the S&P for over 40 years indicates that only 12 have been able to beat the S&P average. With the speed of change we are experiencing today economically, politically, socially and technologically, companies will fade into oblivion or be bought up by another organization unless they are able to reinvent and broaden their focus, as have GE and P&G for example.

When you consider that retail as an industry experiences the highest percentage of corporate failures at all company sizes, longevity doesn't seem to be on their side. Smaller-sized retailers often don't make it past their first five years. Are there lines of separation between the longevity of a retail business and the pursuit of short-term profits? Should we accept that retailing as an industry has only a short-term window of market relevance?

How to Increase Company Longevity

I believe that longevity is possible, provided there is discipline to the way you manage and lead your business. In many businesses, serious fault lines are crossed and the management and boards that run retail companies do not pay enough attention to them. It is the heritage and culture of the brand that makes a significant difference. Protecting these two elements of the business, even with the introduction of programs to improve performance, will yield better results. This does not mean that protecting the wrong culture will bring about better results. It does however mean that an organization with the right set of cultural attributes will likely perform better and longer than others.

In principal, four variables affect the future of a retail business: leadership, innovation, culture, and relevance. Culture seems to be a cornerstone to a healthy long-term business enterprise. For example, GE was founded in 1892 and P&G in 1837. There are four commonalities to the success of these companies and others like them:

1. They are innovators.
2. They have sustainable cultural values.
3. They have incredibly strong succession planning.
4. They know how to grow markets and launch new products and businesses.

Included in these four factors are continuity of leadership and both strategic and organizational purpose.

Alternatively, we hear quite the opposite in organizations that fail: constant change without purpose, personnel changes with each changing of the guard, and competencies and capabilities cast out in favour of a new direction. In turn, many of these new directions cause companies to fail or lose their market position within one to two years. It is possible that these strategies fail even faster with social media communicating dissatisfaction. When you strip away the fabric of a brand's culture, you take away its competitive advantage as well.

Change Management

It is usually the pursuit of the wrong change strategies that cause the greatest level of upheaval and negative impact on the lifecycle of a retail brand. As a process it is the most difficult task to undertake without careful planning. It doesn't matter if your attempting to resuscitate a broken business culture, professionalize an entrepreneurial one or just trying to remain relevant, in my experience each of these has its nuances. While change management initiatives have only one intention to improve the market performance of a company. It also becomes a means for a new or existing leader to invoke their values and control over a brand and that is when failure of change management initiatives occurs the most.

Leadership Changes

At some point in any organization it will be time for a leadership change. However, when the board and owners of a company make the wrong choice it is can be far worse than not making a change.

With new leaders there are personnel changes sometimes they can be excessive ripping away at the fabric of the culture. The key knowledge workers can be found polishing their resumes and exiting on their own, all to the detriment of the retailer. Hiring someone with the wrong skillset can also do as much damage, such as hiring financially or a processed focused leader. Each can put a business through either heavy 'find that penny' cost cutting initiatives or wrap up an organization that needs creativity and innovation into processes that will stymy the culture. If you have to make a leadership change you need to partner with an executive search firm or consultant that will help you define and identify the right traits and characteristics.

Loss of Trust

When companies begin to make changes that are unpopular with consumers and employees, the impact can have significant fallout in trust with all groups. It is extremely important for an executive to understand the intangible value of employee engagement and its impact on the longevity of a company. There is enough evidence to prove that when a company can demonstrate authentic sincerity to train, develop and involve its employees in the growth and challenges a company faces, that you will achieve goals with greater consistency and commitment. Of course that consistency and commitment is translated through customer and stakeholder satisfaction. Yet when trust is breached by a new executive or initiative that is not popular, organizational trouble is not that far behind.

Japan claims to have 20,000 companies that are over 100 years old, according to their records bureau. And there are plenty more in Europe, from Italy to Germany to Spain, with strong, thriving legacies. Perhaps the rest of the world will catch up when we recognize the importance of developing a strong culture and finding ways to sustain it. And as you read this, note that Change Management, Leadership and Trust are some of the reasons why longevity eludes many organizations.

Executive Notes: Some Principles Behind Longevity

When it comes to building a brand's longevity we forget that the fundamental building blocks to success are the same as they are in those organizations that fail. The difference tends to be one of leadership and discipline.

- *Innovation*: Innovative companies are fixated on getting ahead of their competitors, improving existing products and creating new ones. Internally, the organization celebrates the willingness of departments, functions and individuals to find new ways to stay ahead of the competition. Consumers are generally willing to pay a premium for a product or service that is superior in performance and different.

- *Sustainable cultural values:* The best performing organizations have cultures predicated on the changing environment of business. They also involve everyone; for example, executives in these organizations don't come out of their boardrooms pontificating a vision or a "We know best what's good for the organization" attitude. Retailers that do manage change in that manner most certainly will fail. When change strategies fail, it is primarily because someone forgot to involve the very people who work in the company.

- *Leadership:* Nothing is as important as succession planning for leadership at all levels. The continuation of a well-run company and its culture depend on the development and selection of the right leaders along the way. Succession planning must go beyond a list of promotable executives and employees. It must include the ongoing developmental challenges provided for each and the timing that their leadership will be needed.

- *Relevance:* Whether it is the introduction of new store designs, product, markets or channels, retailers with a focus on remaining relevant continually look for the best opportunities for growth. Alternatively, retailers that have failed or are failing did not pursue opportunities to grow their brands in markets and channels that would improve their position and performance.

- *Chart your course:* Without the right culture in place, it is a giant mountain to climb alone. Too often the wrong culture undermines many leaders from realizing their objectives. The performance of organizations is highly dependent on the ability of management to choose the right direction for their organization.

Chapter 3: Evolve or Perish

Principle 3: When change is done properly, it brings to life a culture of innovation and openness that challenges your thinking with an internal eagerness that takes root to continually improve the business' results.

I get concerned when I read that analysts are happy with a retailer whose sales are up by 1.0%. This is inadequate growth when you factor in the increases in the cost of doing business, occupancy, labour and inventory. Sales growth that low does not allow for retail brands to remain sustainable in difficult times. You should also question the increase in sales—how much of it was a price increase? How much can be attributed to excessive discounting and sales promotions? Real growth comes from an increase in traffic counts and transaction growth. Discounting is not a sustainable profit strategy. For example, a recent CNBC report stated that Best Buy has 5 to 10 years of operating life left in them. The commentator also mentioned bookstores and how that business model is a relic of the past. In contrast, Apple wows its customers with their service. Buy their iPad or MacBook and experience it for yourself: the added value is worth the price.

Why Companies Fail

The very premise of success in retail is the ability to innovate in a manner that creates strategic differentiation. When you can achieve that level of strategic focus and deliver on it, you can overcome both competitive and economic challenges. When you consider the number of companies that fail to achieve that objective, you find them restructuring or in bankruptcy. I don't believe that financial lending institutions and private equity firms will lend to or buy defective and dysfunctional retail organizations that lack the depth in competencies and capabilities to grow and evolve their businesses. Based on the number of retailers globally seeking bankruptcy protection from their creditors, there is no doubt that most of them at some point will close their doors.

If you could conduct a post mortem on a failed retail brand, you would note a variety of key issues that lead to their demise:

1. *Wrong strategies* – A lack of competitive intelligence and sophisticated market research can lead to unsuccessful attempts at affecting change. Product and pricing strategies are often not saleable or appropriate for the customer base they are trying to attract.

2. *Disgruntled employees* – Declining sales are followed by poor morale and lower incentives, which cause employee turnover. The stores continue to receive unsalable products, while merchandising practices are confusing with mixed in-store messages and displays. The field leadership acts in fear, making many poor employee relations judgments.

3. *Poor implementation* – Lack of operational experience and project management skills are one issue. Another is ineffective communication – failure to explain instructions in detail for the stores without error and misinterpretation. Product shortages, poor design and fashion selections, poor quality store visuals, and store front displays that lack appeal and draw are other signs of poor implementation.

4. *Poor operational execution* – Lack of in-store and field best practices are a sign of a weak or misdirected field function that is preoccupied or overwhelmed with troubleshooting (performance management, hiring, training, and customer service issues) rather than focused on business development and sales growth.

5. *Dissatisfied customers* – Inconsistent customer service is delivered by untrained retail staff, and this is compounded by a product that doesn't sell and pricing that isn't right. Customers become victims of unproven and failed service and consumer model changes, become frustrated, and never return.

There are usually many signals that something is wrong, and it begins with the organization's leadership misinterpreting either trends or the effectiveness of their strategies. The signs are usually commonplace: excessive inventory from over-ordering or buyers misinterpreting trends. In the end, merchandise is marked down, the number of sales events increase – and in all of this, sales performance is lacking. Marketing initiatives that fail to reach the right consumers, ineffective television advertising, and print that is bundled with 100 other retailers are marketing initiatives that are simply missing the main target. And don't forget digital media marketing, which few retailers have a handle on.

All of this is accompanied by cultural disintegration. Beginning with the reduction of productive retail hours, employee engagement crashes and ultimately customer service and store appearance suffer. At the end of the day, retailers pursue the wrong short-term goals, getting fast strategies to market that destroy many retail brands. Retailers are creating a world of self-service and are asking prices that do not equate with value in the consumer's mind. If customers have to do all the work, how do you convince them to pay a higher price?

So, can anybody do anything right?

Of course retailers can do a lot of the right things the question is how long can they sustain them? And the issues first begin with declining sales followed by shifts in strategy that are not right for either the long or short term. Some of these are captured below and while the list could be longer the following cover off the bigger picture.

Customer Service

The problem with retailers continuing to reduce their employees' hours is that they will be unable to deliver on their service promises. Ultimately, consumers will ask why not buy online, hassle-free. Many retailers struggle with the same issues. At one time customers could enter a DIY store and find someone in every aisle to answer their questions. Today customers have self-checkout counters—not because they save time for the consumer, but because the cost of sustaining the company's business model has reached a point where cost and service are no longer in equilibrium.

If you doubt the impact of service on sales, create a line graph depicting the same store's sales by year versus the number of retail hours used for the same periods. In the same context, consider this: Are your customers served as well today as they were when your brand first started? Productivity gains have always been at the core of adjusting retail hours, however why does an improvement in productivity not always translate into a sales increase?

Innovation and Evolution

No brand, organization or living person has a guaranteed and infinite life cycle unless they recognize the need to evolve. To be clear, it isn't about evolving for the sake of change. It is important to know how to transform and to what, with the intent of remaining competitively relevant.

Even luxury brands have a life cycle. They would lose their appeal if they didn't introduce new designs, technology, and styles every year and for each season. So much of remaining relevant relies on the ability of retailers to sustain their relationship between customers and the founder's values. Accomplish that, and price is no object for consumers in the luxury sector.

Retailers need to be innovative if they want to survive! Innovation is a discipline, and the success of innovative leaders is that they are able to evolve and redefine their strategies well ahead of trends. Instead of following, they create trends with the discipline of an artist. Equally important is they are flawless at implementation and execution.

In more traditional retail (i.e. not luxury goods), the signs that brands are in trouble tend to be visible at the early stages. Solutions often arrive too late in the game, followed by heavy discounting, less service, and deterioration of the brand's overall potential to make a recovery. Yet although we read and hear about these continued mistakes in the news, nothing seems to change. It seems that retail is always at the milking and recovery stage, seldom becoming a brand that will last. The best organizations continue to think about the next demographic of consumers entering the market and how to deliver their value message to them. Planning is at the heart of making each and every transition successful.

Strategic Direction

However, not reacting to changing consumer demographics is not the only issue that brings about the quick death of long standing retail brands. They also suffer at the hands of strategic direction, usually poorly thought-out strategies that tend to be implemented and delivered in an equally poor way.

Every year numerous retail businesses file for bankruptcy protection around the world. The numbers will likely jump even higher during the next five years. Retailers will continue to succumb to competition and a shift in consumer preferences. At the heart of it lies the very talent pool that manages these businesses. Why? Because many are unable to recognize trends fast enough to adapt and make a compelling enough challenge for change in their supply chain, designs, pricing, store designs, training, and cost management. Organizations that have a strong presence in the market place and are able to adapt usually have developed flexible business models and have learned to evolve their strategies quickly. They will be the long-term survivors.

The following may sound counterintuitive, especially for those who follow their graduate school teachings. You know that strategies have to be adhered to, and everyone along the value chain needs to be part of the success model. The challenge is that this kind of thinking can get you caught up in the wrong direction and feed the wrong strategies. Today's retail field is like open water filled with sharks that are more nimble and know what it takes to survive. The old rules simply no longer apply. Winning is going to take a lot more flexibility, knowing that your current path may only be good enough for a couple of years or less.

Change is the Only Constant

Many of us who have spent time on overseas assignments understand all too well what discontinuities are all around us. Nothing in business is a sacred cow and change is the only constant. I believe that today's retail market place in North America, Europe, and Asia Pacific for that matter, are all in a phase of discontinuity. The same can be said about many segments of the retail industry. Simply put, any retail segment that can sell online at lower prices and use mail or low-cost courier services to deliver a product to consumers makes all similar bricks and mortar players vulnerable to change. No one will be exempt from the inevitable impact of this shift.

Why are retail businesses so vulnerable? The most obvious answer is that their investment in their brick and mortar stores exceeds the available demand and capacity required to serve the consumers interested in their retail concept. However, retailers cannot ignore the reasons for pending business failure, the inability to build their online revenue, ineffective strategies, an out-dated consumer model, poor marketing and merchandising practices, the power of social media, a new level of consumerism, and a lack of employee engagement. All of these forces are constantly at play and it will require a strong leadership team to address them consecutively. Yet again these issues are not only endemic to retail only, countless industries are struggling with two or more of these barriers.

Executive Notes: Why Evolution is Important

I have found that speed is now as important as the availability of information was 30 years ago. Especially when it comes down to understanding the need for change and then how to accomplish that successfully.

1. There are three fundamental reasons why your brand needs to evolve:
    1.1 The growth of online models
    1.2 Fast changing consumer preferences
    1.3 Disruptive market entrants

2. Leadership must be quick to respond to change and to effectively execute the right strategies.

3. Is your organization wired for continuous improvement and are the change initiatives working?

Chapter 4: The Global Retail Challenges

PRINCIPLE 4: BUILD A RETAIL brand with a global perspective.

Retailers around the world have taken it on the chin, and in a slow economy analysts know the risks retailers face with such low numbers. What is on everyone's mind? Figuring out how long they'll have to wait before it all rebounds. As the recovery continues to be delayed, the vulnerability index (if there were such a measure) for minor and major retailer's increases with each passing day. After three plus years in Asia I learned that success as many found was not as simple as setting up a store front and waiting for Asia's higher end consumers to coming in and shop. There are numerous challenges facing retailers that wish to expand in emerging markets and as much as the draw is enticing you need to have a team and the long-term financial resources to see you through the growth cycle. And it is equally important that you forget about what you know of the retail industry as consumers shop differently and in some instances will negotiate for price. While in other foreign markets consumers are considered treasure seekers looking for the best deal. In my experience forget everything you know about todays world in North America and start thinking about how retail and consumerism was developing in the 1960's that is more of what you will encounter. And as for the precious affluent nouveau riche of the emerging markets, you may want to reconsider their impact on your business as they are the new jet setters traveling around the world and shopping outside of their home country. The real bounty lies with the emerging middle class. However, to attract them your product and price offerings must have a local fare or you will have more browsers than buyer's as price disparity with purchasing power is a significant opportunity today.

Global Retail Issues

In my research for this book, I found that retailers around the world have commonalities, some of which are country-specific and others which are global. The top five global issues are of no surprise to anyone in this industry:

1. *Online and technology* – The pervasiveness of these disruptive business models are being felt everywhere and their impact is unique. They are threatening everything. The more interesting point is that retailers are building online platforms that are not strong enough to make them revenue growth vehicles out of concern that they will impact their offline stores.

2. *Slower demand* – Job growth is slow, banking conditions are even worse, and austerity measures are taking their toll. It seems the wealthy leisure society that was promised with the advancement of technology was a fallacy. And as a result of these challenges more retailers are faced with financial distress, which has lead some into bankruptcy or financial restructures. That in turn ends up with smaller organizations and perhaps less able to command a strong market performance.

3. *Changing demographics* – With an aging population, the number of higher-end consumers is diminishing. Younger consumers are being influenced by digital media and many retailers haven't figured out how to leverage that fact. In addition, retailers are not moving fast enough to adapt. And what about the boomers? They are healthy, wealthy, living longer, and technically competent, yet belong to an underserved demographic. Everyone is chasing the younger, smaller, and more price-sensitive demographics.

4. *Cost management* – Whether it's occupancy, inventory, or payroll, the cost of running a bricks and mortar business continues to erode profits. As for payroll cuts, stores feel them the most, and followed by sales and service suffering. We all know the cost benefit of manufacturing in Asia is slowly eroding, with wages and other operating expenses increasing creates added pressure on retail pricing.

5. *Foreign Competition* – The entry of a new competitor does not guarantee it instant success. Not surprisingly, both sides are struggling today: those who are expanding internationally and those competing against them locally. The competitive collision course will be hardest for those further from home and with fewer local resources. Retailers with satellite offices in foreign countries simply do not maximize their opportunities for growth and trade off a larger share for what they believe is a cost savings.

Country – and Continent-Specific Retail Issues

In addition, each continent and country has its own challenges in the retail sector.

United States:

- Diminishing high-end consumer base
- Slow domestic growth
- Lack of effectiveness at international expansion
- Disruptive online models
- Oversaturated and aging shopping centres
- Expansion into countries like Canada with just a regional office has proven imminently short-sighted and leads many to miss their full business potential. Trying to run Canada as an extended market of the USA has proven to be ineffective in employee relations and customer retention.

Canada:

- Canadian dollar at parity with the US
- Pervasive cross-border shopping

- Foreign competitors entering the market
- Slow to compete online
- Unable to effectively move internationally

Europe:

- Economic uncertainty
- Austerity measures
- Severe recessions in some countries
- Changing demographics
- Unemployment

Australia:

- Online shopping not being pursued by retailers
- Entry of foreign competitors
- Retailers unable to launch international expansion
- Some of the highest mortgage rates in the world

China:

- Foreign retailers not realizing the promise of profit growth
- A long-term play, and longer if prices aren't local
- Slowing economy
- Luxury buyers don't shop locally
- Local retail chains expanding faster
- Occupancy costs astronomical for foreigners
- Empty shopping centres

India:

- Fragmented retail market
- Regulated and Protected
- Unsophisticated retail development
- Still a decade away for international retailers
- More culturally challenging than China

Responding to Economic Issues

Retailers face a serious gap between achieving stronger performances and being relevant in an environment that is quickly changing. The economic marketplace isn't the healthiest, and many are only posting comparable sales growth of 0.5 – 1.5%, which isn't enough to meet the issue of rising costs.

Over the last 10 years, retailers have reduced non-productive labour hours, highlighting improvements in technology or eliminating redundant tasks that have affected stores. All of that made sense; however the pressure on wages continues and what is left are productive hours. As prices continue to rise and transactions begin to decline, productive hours have come down precipitously. In effect, hours have continued to come down to a point where many have created a self-service reality. This has occurred in an industry that needs service to increase conversion and satisfy customers and grow volume.

Retailers have lost their edge in service and have inadvertently given way to the disruptive powers of change. No one can argue the need to manage costs, however what many financial decisions didn't factor in was that the productivity increases needed in terms of higher transactions by each retail employee never materialized. As a result, many of the changes the industry has been forced to deal with have been self-inflicted.

Retail is now going through 'creative destruction' – it cannot be stopped and it has to be embraced. If retailers fail to recognize the signals and timing for change in their own retail brands, they will face the same deterioration and failure that others have.

A Changing Business Model

In their book Creative Destruction, Foster and Kaplan suggest that organizations locked into their own cultural beliefs may not recognize that a better business model has been developed elsewhere. In fact, we have all seen the number of failed retailers who were so immersed in their own traditional beliefs about "advantages of scale, market power, consumer knowledge and financial resources" that they didn't think it possible that another retailer could intrude in their secure world until it was too late.

When you consider all of the above, retail as an industry is in a serious period of change. Whether it is a bricks and mortar competitor or an online game changer, the failure to evolve rests with the retailer (the CEO and the board) that missed the opportunity to capitalize on what would be the next big strategy for their company. The key strategic issue retailers need to address is, are they leading change in their organizations, or are they merely reacting to it? And how will they sustain a culture of innovation to remain relevant?

The predominant reason to pursue a change strategy is to shake up an organization and reignite stronger market share and financial performance. However, when change initiatives do not materialize the desired results, the negative impact on the culture and performance of the retailer can be more severe than its previous position. This creates a catalyst for more change initiatives which includes replacing leadership and returning to once abandoned strategies.

A retail organization that is in need of a change in performance needs to consider its approach and the impact on employees, customers, and business partners before it embarks on its new journey.

Aside from what has already been covered off to this point, performance improvement programs anywhere in the world will require internal transparency and a very strong understanding of external competitive forces before they can launch effective growth strategies.

International Expansion

The subject of international expansion is another debate. However, retailers that are building their international presence in Asia, South America, and other parts of the world are faced with competitive challenges that are unique to the country. Each country has its own nuances and there are obstacles to expansion. The first mistake retailers make with international expansion is the assumption that they will shape the market. The second is that consumers will be excited about a new consumer model. Third is that they are entering the market with a relevant brand and a demand with the right price and product offerings. The home improvement market in China, for example, has not achieved the consumer attention and demand that was hoped for. The many Chinese that have bought new homes, primarily condominiums, do not have the financial means to spend beyond their current investment. Many of the opportunities in developing markets are about timing with the right level of demand. International success is a long-term objective for many and a healthy capital investment. In addition to this, achieving mass appeal can also be very expensive such as negotiating leases in Asia the average terms are 2-3 years and automatic renewals are seldom available.

Many retailers do not recognize the enormity of successfully developed international brands entering their country. They have sharpened their skills in such a manner that they first understand the host market and the potential growth based on the demand and appeal that their brand has in this new market place. Regrettably not all retailers understand what it takes to succeed in a foreign market such as those destined to start up in Canada between 2013-2014.

On the other hand many of the local retailers have also enjoyed such a blissful existence with nominal competitive challenges that everything they knew about retailing and competition is about to change permanently.

The best example is that of Target launching in Canada during 2013. Many local national retail chains have been preparing with new advertising campaigns attempting to highlight Canadian loyalty. The reality may be a somewhat different as consumers will be the ones who choose where their loyalties lie and which retailers will benefit from it. Many retailers that missed the opportunity to improve their relevance with consumers over last five years will likely experience serious contractions to their business.

At the end of the day, to have chosen a strategy that would lead your brand to sustain market relevance before competitive threats arrived would have been a wiser choice. To simply respond with discounts and sales will only delay the need to change and prevent failure that time is likely 18-36 months away for many as in the case above once Target enters Canada.

Executive Notes: Learning from other Global Retailers is Important

- How vulnerable is your brand to competitive threats local and global ones?
- Embrace change as part of your culture.
- Develop breakaway strategies.
- Build flexibility into your organization.
- Don't ignore the nuances and needs of operating your foreign operations with the right level of resources to maximize growth.
- Build your domestic business with a sound foundation before you think about international expansion.
- Constantly look for ways to refresh your position in the market place.

Priority II: Embrace Change - Define the Opportunities

EARLY IN MY CAREER I learned that in retail, change is the only thing that is predictable. The only other thing that you can predict is that if you make no changes, someone else is going to take your share of the market from you.

Boards and companies change leadership when they recognize that a new leader is needed to reinvent a business and/or to get it back on track. For the most part, reinventing your business to be relevant in the market place is a key priority. The main strategic goal of most retailers is simply to grow market share, profits and shareholder value. All of these are important in the marketplace, unfortunately the pursuit of short-term results also puts a different set of changes in motion that at times retailers cannot recover from.

Chapter 5: Why Retailers Fail – One Retailer's Tale

PRINCIPLE 5: ALWAYS EXPECT THAT your brand will face adversity. The speed with which you correctly or incorrectly address internal and external threats will be the real story.

According to the Centre for Retail Research, between the years 2007 and the first half of 2012, 208 retail companies in the United Kingdom filed for Administration (the US's version of Chapter 11) of course chapter 11 in its simplest definition is a means to stave off bankruptcy and get enough time to work out terms with creditors. In other words, over 21,000 retail locations were affected and 186,000 potential jobs were lost. In Canada, the retail trade is the second highest contributor to bankruptcies in business. Statistics Canada reports that in 2007, 895 retailers filed for bankruptcy. In the US, 1.1 million retail stores occupy over 14.2 billion square feet of space. This shows an oversaturated market with resulting continuous Chapter 11 filings every year.

The principles of failure seem to be universal in the retail industry, and usually everything that can go wrong in many of these failed companies does go wrong, and very quickly. There is a cycle to this. As you follow along, you may catch a glimpse of your own business at some stage. If you don't, then you are one of the lucky few – at least for now.

The Cycle of Failed Companies

Here is a scenario about a fictitious retail company. They have been holding their own for a number of years. However, changes in their segment of the industry have led to aggressive price competition with discounters and online players cutting into the market. They've been slow with the development of their online business, and the last couple of years have taken their toll on the business.

Scene One: Trouble is Brewing

The retailer begins to recognize that consumers are not buying the products they have on their shelves. The feedback from the stores tends to be concerns over colours, styles, and brands. This is followed by the retailer selling some of the unsalable product to third party liquidators. The next round of product comes in and it still isn't moving. Additional feedback from customers and employees alike gets collected; management hears that the product is fine, but price-wise the value doesn't match their competitors'. Customers say that they can get something similar for less at another retailer. Management's response to the situation is increased sales offers and select product markdowns. They also add a store incentive for employees to move the product out faster.

The discussions during the senior management meetings are that consumers are pulling back in general. Members of the executive team repeat some news update from the business networks that supports this interpretation. That information provides both a little peace of mind to the retailer that they are not alone, and a belief that soon the market will rebound. At the end of each meeting the CEO tells everyone that they have the right product and offers in place, they just have to get their store teams to work a little harder on conversion. For the layman conversion can be measured in one of many ways however the most common is as follows:

The number of buyers divided by the number of customers who visit the store = Customer Conversion.

Scene Two: Management's Obsessions

Unfortunately, two months into the new plan, the hoped-for turnaround has not occurred, and the pressure is on to cut costs and make the most out of a bad situation. By this time the rhetoric on the economic climate has stopped as a few key retailers posted very strong earnings in their most recent quarter.

At the next meeting, the CEO proclaims that while the economy is generally flat, key retailers are posting very strong results. He further states that he is not happy with his team's performance and by next week expects each functional leader to come in with a plan to accomplish three things: reduce costs, grow sales, and make up the profit shortfall for the year.

Scene Three: The Spiral

Jamie has been a field manager for over ten years and he's never seen things in such disarray. Communication from home office has been inconsistent, and the weekly updates which have needed improvement for many years have gone from poor to worse. In every store that Jamie has been visiting, store managers complain about their staff's hours being cut and incentives being drastically reduced. One manager told Jamie that if she couldn't get her incentives back up she would have to leave, as the incentives bridged the cost of her kids being at daycare.

Jamie himself is pretty tired of the whole situation. He thinks back to the job offer he got six months ago. When he gets home he tells his wife that it feels like the beginning of the end; he feels that all they are doing is reacting to sales trends, and it doesn't seem like they have a plan on how to get out of it. And to top off his day, his boss calls to say that Jamie's performance is not meeting expectations and he wants Jamie to come in for a discussion tomorrow.

Scene Four: Catalyst of Your Own Demise

After several weeks of Mondays rehashing the previous week's results, the senior management team is called in to an important meeting on Friday morning. The chair of the board arrives and the CEO announces his resignation. He begins with, "After almost eight years I have decided to move on and allow someone else to take the reins and see us through to the next generation of growth." The new CEO is introduced and promises everyone that he will work closely with them to improve the performance of the organization.

Monday, which everyone hopes will be a new day and beginning, passes with everyone getting used to the new boss's style. For the first few months everything is fine. By the end of the fourth quarter, the new CEO comes to the meeting announcing that he has been working with the board and they have decided that the organization needs to go through a cultural transformation if it is to survive into the next generation. Within days, announcements are made on the hour every hour. It is clear that there will be a new executive team very soon. With the changes come new processes and procedures. Management is very focused on execution, and the next obvious place for change is store operations.

Scene Five: Timing

Jamie has been getting along well with his new boss. He is delivering on all the new procedures that were put into place but sales are still struggling, and even with new products and new pricing strategies, the traffic isn't coming in. Today is also a big day for Jamie—he is celebrating his 11th year with the company and his new boss is coming to see him. He and Jamie get into a discussion about culture: where they are and where they want to go next. That's when Jamie is hit with the news that the role of the field manager is going to change and he is no longer needed on the team.

Scene Six: Fear and the Second Quarter

Members of the executive team meet quietly on their own. There is a great deal of concern that many of them have left good jobs behind. Business results have not changed and the CEO doesn't seem to be able to provide enough guidance or direction. Sales are stable and negative to the previous year. The bleeding has stopped, but a lot of competent people have left and gone to work for the company's competitors.

Scene Seven: Another Beginning

At the end of the third quarter, a morning meeting is planned. The chair arrives early and greets everyone as usual. It is 9:00 a.m. and the CEO is not in the room. The chair stands up and clears his throat, stating that he and the board of directors asked the CEO to leave and that a search would be conducted to find his successor.

Why Do Retailers Fail?

I was once told an old Swedish saying: "The death of one man is bread and butter for another." That pretty much summarizes the reality in business. We press our resources and people so hard, then blame them for the lack of or bad management decisions.

Retail organizations fail for several reasons, some mentioned in previous chapters:

- Lack of the right strategic choices
- Ineffective change management
- Poor leadership
- Missed market opportunities
- Unnecessary surgical eradication of cultures
- Lack of accountability
- Risk-adverse and reluctance to change

The problem with the CEOs depicted in the scenario, and I am sure that you picked up on it, is that they employed the two worst leadership styles. The first was a longer-term leader who believed that he understood the business and industry and was willing to try all the old tricks to get everything back on track. The second was good at orchestrating the movement of change, meaning that he was the type that didn't spend enough time with understanding the issues or sharing his vision of the future with the organization. New leaders coming into this role tend to surround themselves with their old guard from a past life so that they can protect their position. The right leader for a significant change initiative is as important as the change strategies being pursued. Regrettably, that is not how all owners and corporate boards take part in the oversight of an organization facing dramatic shifts in direction.

What we all recognize here is that change for the sake of change doesn't work. And when you do have to change, if there isn't enough candour and clear strategic direction coupled with new strategies, it will be like the character Jamie said: "It doesn't seem like we have a plan on how to get out of it."

Is it possible that all the things that went wrong in this vignette could happen in one organization? I certainly hope not, although, for each defunct company that has failed, I believe that the employees internally may have a similar or worse tale to share with us.

Executive Notes: Managing the Future of your Brand

- How can you best embrace the organization to create change?
- What information are you missing that prevents you from guiding your organization on the right course?
- What are the short-term wins you can get in the next 90 days to demonstrate your management team's conviction to winning in the market place?
- How do you need to change personally as a leader so that you are not part of the problem?
- How does your management team build confidence within the organization that change is healthy and necessary?
- How do you manage the fallout of change more effectively and humanely?
- Where are you with corporate social responsibility and employee engagement?
- Who do you need to call upon internally as advocates to inspire employees at all levels of the organization?

Chapter 6: Pursuing the Wrong Strategies

PRINCIPLE 6: AS A CEO, your role is to leave a viable brand behind for the next generation of leaders to grow.

The Titanic was called the ship of ships and the most venerable and unsinkable marvel mankind had built. Yet the captain and crew were not paying attention to changes in their sea-faring environment when the ship sunk. In the same way, when businesses fail to pay attention to their environment and strategic choices, the iceberg they run into is just as damaging.

Many retailers struggle with growing their customer base, and the majority do not achieve the level of repeat business that they would like to have. We all want to grow our businesses from the inside out, yet when we ignore the obvious competitive forces, businesses and industries can face disruptive changes or even extinction. Businesses and leaders have not overcome myopia, and many remain unaware of how swift the competitive forces in this industry can derail their performance and market position.

Of particular note is the speed with which consumer's opinions and preferences are being forged by the speed of technology and the availability of information, which shapes and moves consumers to another retailer's competitors or abandon products because of their social interests. As a result, by not being connected to the right information internally and externally, a retailer can weaken their strategic choices or worse discovering they launched the wrong strategies.

Top Five Reasons why Strategies Fail

In my opinion, strategies fail for five specific reasons:

1. Lack of consumer research
2. Inadequate competitive intelligence
3. Undeliverable service promises
4. Ineffective change programs
5. Poor technological leadership

An effective strategic plan is like a custom made suit if you don't use a tailor and just buy a pattern and make it yourself the finished product will not have the same appeal. Unfortunately, many strategies are not tailor-made and the strategies that are developed internally miss the mark in many respects and usually it is the same resources interjecting and rehashing the same ideas. Strategies do need to be home grown although when sales are down and you are losing share to the same internal thinking you must revisit your options.

Lack of Consumer Market Research – The right level of research, targeted to understanding consumer behaviour toward existing products or services or those that need to be defined and developed, is essential in good business management. Without effective market research, you can pursue the wrong strategies, media initiatives, service models, and product lines. Consider this: if your competitor's market share in the category you serve is greater than yours and you are outspending them in media dollars, then there is a definite issue with strategic choices. Does this happen? Of course it does!

Often when you read about an organization that is struggling or has failed, it is likely that decisions were left solely to internal thinking and consumer information that has been rehashed and is outdated. These practices often become stale and lead to unproductive and missed opportunities for real growth. Organizations that rely entirely on their own internal business intelligence to grow sales and market share are likely missing 50% of their goals. Why? Generally, most don't spend enough time reviewing the external environment, how to respond to current and potential threats or opportunities that are developing in the marketplace.

Motorola was once conducting a consumer feedback session with younger consumers. Throughout the session, Motorola knew that this was an emerging customer base for them. During the session, a young man spoke up and asked, "Does the cell phone come in any other colour than black?" The Motorola marketers who were attending the session behind cameras were shocked at the revelation and that it was so simple. It didn't require the introduction of new technology or features; it was simply about personalizing the phones to the customer's own colour preferences.

Inadequate Competitive Intelligence – Retailers track the offers and advertising efforts of their competitors, however few actually dissect the information and understand it. Collecting this data cannot be ignored, especially in price-driven markets. Competitive intelligence answers two major questions for business leaders: Does your competitor have an inherent advantage or weakness that you can exploit? Who collects the competitive data and what is done with it? In other words, is there an internal report that assesses the current situation?

Many organizations either don't collect competitive data or simply stop their people from talking about it. Often this is driven by the internal business belief that their brand is better than others and will win if they work hard enough at it. Some organizations that do collect this information do not have someone dedicated to providing a regular summary of key changes in the market that may affect business or identifying underserved markets and emerging opportunities. What you do with this information is far more important than collecting it.

When competitive intelligence gathering is not mandated from the CEO, there will be no value in it. Marketing teams sometimes dismiss the information as distracting from their core strategies. In fact, the opposite is true: changes in competitive strategies and tactics identify whether your business or someone else's is changing a competitor's direction and influencing consumer preferences.

Undeliverable Service Promises – An often overlooked aspect of assessing internal strategy is the company's ability to deliver on its service promise. Whether it is about a delivery time, quality, product performance, or a personalized level of service, it is sometimes assumed in the retail world that expectations have been met because a sale has been made. Your delivery of service will only be as good as your execution. Retail organizations need to follow operational standards to ensure flawless execution.

I have found that many retailers are reluctant to be stringent in their operational practices and allow their teams to have their own set of performance standards, sometimes developed by region or by the field manager. In essence, the entire organization has multiple agendas and focuses that risk not being aligned with the overall business strategy. Without proper checks and balances in place, such as measurable operational standards, store visits alone will not define strengths and opportunities.

The second part of this is pursuing a service model that cannot be executed in today's environment. Included in this statement are the competencies, attitudes, and behaviours of your employees. Retail companies need to be especially preoccupied with service as an advantage to grow their business. Without boilerplate service procedures, specialty retailers and department stores are going to miss their sales targets.

Ineffective Change Programs – To remain competitive, the right change management initiatives always need to be pursued with the long-term health of the organization in mind. Change management practices can and do get in the way of competitive efforts, especially if they are misaligned with corporate strategies. When change management initiatives are not corporately directed and do not have the right organizational DNA imprinted on them, they generally fail. The majority of organizations that struggle with change management do so because they have lost their own identity and the clarity of what needs to be achieved.

All too often, the signs of misguided change management include:

i. Allowing the book-of-the-month club to filter into managing your culture. (From time to time a new idea or thinking comes along that is fashionable and it seems that everyone thinks this is the new wave that will change the world, improve the workplace and performance. It doesn't happen that way, in fact these ideas merely get in the way of the culture you want to run.)

ii. Using unapproved training programs (Everyone should have a process for new ways to train or what to train to be filtered, considered and perhaps approved. When that doesn't happen things at the store levels can become very muddy.)

iii. Attempting to adopt another organization's cultural practices. (Quite often with a new hire on board you will find some trying to employ their own past cultural beliefs and experience which may be counter to your business. You will need to manage that if it is not a good fit.)
iv. Pursuing external programs that are destroying company morale and trust (This is likely the worst of all scenarios adopting systems or practices that are counterintuitive to your business and if unaware a senior leadership team could find themselves fighting plenty of internal fires.)

There must be a gatekeeper who, with the guidance of upper management, oversees and assesses the impact of every initiative brought forward. This should include:

i. Having a clear view of how you want your organization to work at managing your competitive strategy
ii. Having a vision of what you want the outcome to look and act like behaviourally in your organization
iii. Not allowing any external cultural ideas to influence your culture
iv. Establishing unwavering service attitude
v. Making change an acceptable aspect of the culture, and even an expectation
vi. Gaining employee buy-in through strong internal communication of the how, why and benefits of change
vii. Paying honest attention to the feedback and questioning what you don't have enough information on

Poor Technological Leadership – Most of us have heard of Moore's Law. Simply stated, it says that the number of microprocessor transistors on integrated circuits doubles every two years. Between 1971 and 2011, they grew from 2,300 to 2.6 billion. Fortunately, business does not evolve as fast – at least not yet. Although technology within the retail industry is making strides, it is also changing the way we do business.

Today, organizations need leaders who can assess the competitive climate, read the internal data and make very quick decisions on product, pricing, and promotional efforts.

Technological innovations, such as social networking, mobile devises with augmented realities, and e-commerce are all here to stay. All of these will continue to evolve, and if retail leaders do not embrace this change, many will face inevitable extinction.

I also contend that the failure caused by poor product and merchandising decisions is driven by our inability or unwillingness to leverage technology effectively enough to make the right decisions. Certainly, technology is used to read sales data and determine which product styles, designs, and colours are being sold. However, all of this is after the fact and is a lag indicator. Retailers need to embrace technology beyond reading sales data and supporting an e-commerce channel that doesn't generate sales. The speed of technology is evolving and the use of it by consumers is also accelerating with smartphones, tablets, and the advancement of mobile payments, all of which are game changers to the industry. Yet there are retailers who have not invested in large enough data lines in their stores to speed up both service and their own data collection.

Technological leadership is not only important in its ability to capture more sales and grow your customers – it also plays a role in retaining your staff. There is no greater recruitment tool than the use of current technology to serve customers. It will be harder to recruit and retain staff, and ask them to deliver a higher level of productivity, when the technology in your store is so outdated that they can barely get to the next customer.

In retail, it is no longer a choice: you are either serving with technology that meets the expectations of this generation, or you are accelerating your brand toward becoming irrelevant.

Staying relevant is a subject of further discussion in chapter 15, however without understanding the reasons for failure and being cognizant of them at all times, a chain or independent retailer cannot prevent the risks from overwhelming them and quickly.

Executive Notes: Every Decision is a Link and it Matters

- Build strategic organizational disciplines.
- Know your market and your competitors.
- Your biggest mistake will always be pursuing strategies without the right competencies.
- Product and marketing strategies will be your weakest links when you have the wrong information.
- Allow for inquisitiveness but challenge the thinking and direction.
- The next evolution should always be on every executive's priorities and performance review.
- Invest in leading internally with customer information.

Chapter 7: The Dilemma of Online versus Offline – Part One

PRINCIPLE 7: YOUR MARKETING AND strategy teams need to think beyond the reaches of their offline stores. The new economy is pushing for virtual stores to the mix, and retailers need to bring this concept to life. Redefine your business as a disruptive retail brand with a commitment to technology, developing the abilities to deliver the right products and services more efficiently, and create new market opportunities.

During the last five years, retailers have struggled through some interesting challenges that reflect both the economy and consumers as a whole. In the not too distant past, disruptive retailers were big box and outlet stores. Then, shopping shifted from malls to open-air power centres, which are conveniently located near large or growing communities. In addition to national and regional chains, independent store owners also had the opportunity to open in these centres, unlike malls where independents found it difficult to break in with their new business models.

Online Business Models

Today, the meaning of disruptive has shifted once again. This time, disruptive business models have begun to redefine and reshape entire categories within retail. Online business models are changing the way consumers shop, in many instances for much lower prices. There are no exclusions to this unnerving competition. Everything from food, auto parts, and books to music, clothing, and accessories are all being sold online. Even products once viewed as controlled, such as eyewear and medicine, are also being challenged in the online marketplace.

This phenomenon is driven by entrepreneurs themselves. Perhaps they were once traditional retailers, suppliers, or consumers who are now saying "There has to be a better way!" These entrepreneurs have another advantage. If their business and consumer model is right, they can stake a claim to a share of the market over night. There is more to this potential threat. For the first time, independent retailers are able to market online and build a platform that competes against larger retailers. This is a shift in retailing. As new models begin to unfold, they will chip away at established chains. Traditional chains will continue to lose because they are not as fast at deploying their vision of the future as other competitors who are not constrained by fear or barriers, real or perceived.

I was recently invited to a retail conference with a number of store leaders attending. The theme was change and the importance of technology. I was surprised – not by the subject, but rather that the question of whether or not you should expand your online retail business into a revenue generator was still being debated.

Retailers that are waiting for the opportune moment to launch their online strategies (and other disruptive models) may find themselves in the game far too late. It is understandable that many want to protect their offline (bricks and mortar) investments, however the truth is that time may be their biggest enemy.

Developing a Disruptive Business Model

How do you turn your brand into a disruptive business model that sets the stage for growth in share, sales, and profits? While many retailers are still trying to protect their traditional turf, those who want to be relevant need to break away from the herd. What will make you different from the competition has to be unique enough that your brand has a following of retailers and consumers who respect your brand. Apple and Lululemon are good examples of that today.

It is not enough to just to have the best price, as price is not in itself a differentiator. Having a disruptive model will require a change in your positioning and the flexibility to transform your business from a follower of trends to one that defines them. Once again, I point out that the main purpose of this book is to show how important it is to remain relevant in an unpredictable and competitive market.

Global experience has shown that retailers that remain competitive, and are able to sustain a relevant market position, tend to be more entrepreneurial in their DNA. They are not fixated on what has worked in the past. They continuously seek and develop new products, services, and marketing strategies to ensure their differentiation in the market place. Entrepreneurship is an inherent characteristic of these organizations. Everyone's commitment to the success of the organization is tied to strong values and cultures. In addition, they understand the importance of speed: that is, being fast and effective at launching a business model that works.

One common misunderstanding that executives in today's economy fail to grasp is that disruptive forces (business models) are constantly being developed. Unless you are doing the same, new competitors will be at your door eroding your market share, sales, and profits. An organization's life cycle will only be as long as its value proposition remains strong and relevant. If retailers are unable to embrace the idea of change in their organizations, they will fail to sustain their current position in the market place.

However, having an online platform is only the beginning of the experience the offline store itself needs to be just as commanding of attention. The use of technology to impress consumers is going to arrive rather quickly. In fact as of late I began to question why we bother with paper visuals and continuously struggle with creative costs, shipping to stores, and coordinating consistency in displays when retailers who want to save money could easily incorporate digital signs controlling their front door visuals and messaging at the press of a button from their home office.

However, technology needs to be further embraced in store to improve service and the customer's experience. Service needs to be reinvented with the use of technology as a key driver but not with the intent to just decrease overall payroll costs. Each retailer will have to determine their own strategy, yet when we visit department and specialty stores, there are aisles of product, less staff, and a sea of price points with nothing or no one to help the consumer make the right buying decision.

All of this is a solvable problem provided the brand is relevant and wants to continue to stay that way. The risks of doing nothing outweigh the risks of trialing new ideas to improve your customers shopping experience. I would not be surprised if the use of technology can keep your customers browsing in your stores longer.

It is true that online retailing has its share of failures and that isn't surprising. Although, chains have the opportunity to dominate this channel provided that they can manage their supply chain and drive down delivery costs.

An online business needs to be focused on capturing new customers from markets where demand for your brand is currently low or the cost of entering that market is prohibitive at this time. I do not believe that all retailers look at online as an opportunity for growth I believe that they see it as a challenge to their internal capabilities. What we have to ask ourselves is how many retailers could have staved restructures and bankruptcy had they looked at how to leverage new channels.

There are many retailers who still doubt that the online world will be that much of a threat because consumers by nature like to shop in person and browse stores. While the latter is true, the media is littered with columns about retailers who have become showrooms for online retailers. And we should expect more of that to continue. The main question is what do you do about it?

Is show-rooming a passing phenomenon or a cause of growth from on-line retailers? This important competitive challenge began to take root first and obviously in the USA because they are much further along with disruptive on-line retail threats than in other countries.

Consider for a moment why show-rooming has taken root. An on-line retailer in essence has the ability to deliver a product for a lower price than off-line retailers. Consumers know this so they begin their price comparisons which now include on-line retail price and shipping versus pickup at a retailer with potentially instant gratification. Retailers should get use to show-rooming as an addition to consumer comparison shopping.

The answer is simply that until off-line retailers get their pricing and product aligned in both channels show-rooming will not decrease as a threat. I use the word decrease because I don't believe that it will ever go away.

The executive challenge is to develop or hire a marketing team that understands how to create online strategies that will grow your brand and drive awareness. Certainly everyone has a web page that's the easy part the difficulty comes into making it a revenue generator for your brand. It will not become an important vehicle to grow your sales unless it has a regimented focus and that includes asking about last week's revenue every Monday morning. And that includes setting sales goals that are over and above your offline store performance. Some retailers are very good at setting those goals unfortunately their strategies to grow online revenue doesn't match their focus and therein lies the major problem. Others are still hesitant because of a lack of execution to knowledge on how to operate their online business effectively and congruent to their offline (brick and mortar) business.

What will in my opinion get in the way of existing retailers are entrepreneurs who have broken the code on pricing, cost, service and customer experience to attract and retain customers.

Executive Notes: Lead in your Segment of the Market

- Determine how you can break away from the rest in your category.
- Think through which elements of technology are right for your business.
- Reinvent service by leveraging technology.
- How can you become a disruptive retailer with the competencies and capabilities you have today?
- What needs to change organizationally?
- The use of digital visual displays can lower your costs and enhance your overall brand image.
- Are you aware of the new players that have entered your segment of the industry?
- Look outside your industry for inspiration and innovation.

Chapter 8: The Dilemma of Online versus Offline – Part Two

PRINCIPAL 8: IN THE OLD economy, it was about how many points of distribution (stores) you had. In the new economy, it's about how you incorporate a virtual store (online) into the mix and keep reaching for more customers.

The third 'P' in marketing, as we all know, is 'place' as a reminder product and price are number one and two with promotion in fourth place.' Retail has had an exemplary period of growth during the last 30 years. It has been very much an inflationary period in which developers and investors wanted retailers to add many more stores. During that time, store growth was the only strategic option to growing your sales and building brand presence. Store growth is a larger question today: just how many locations does a retailer need to remain competitive and sustain their brand presence without giving up sales and profits? While developers and the financial markets want retailers to expand at a faster rate, is that a sustainable model in today's market place? Can a retailer achieve strong sales growth, brand presence, and demand with fewer stores? I believe that they can, provided that they have a central e-commerce model upon which to build their sales and profits.

e-Commerce

There should no longer be a debate about whether or not to build a strong e-commerce platform; all retailers have to find a way to bridge that gap. I refer to this as "crossing the gap," with the gap being that the third "P" now should also include the virtual store (online) rather than just bricks and mortar (offline). The offline world is faced with choices, one of them being how to better serve customers and retain them. It is no longer just about who has the most stores; it is about who will have the best complete model. Within that model, successful retailers will have the best mix of online and offline strategies, reaching more customers with their stores. The offline stores will represent the best in class with respect to service, merchandising, and overall customer experience.

Today, retailers are either online or offline operators. They may dabble in both, but only one represents their core business and profits. Retailers that will struggle the most with making a ventured leap into crossing the gap will be those that operate as a franchise or in a dealer network. Unless their agreements provide the franchisor with complete autonomy over marketing and product strategic choices, this will be a tough one for them to overcome.

Most e-commerce platforms have a great deal of company information embedded on their site: sales events, product availability, and minor ordering opportunities. However, the majority have not made their new and future revenue generator online. I believe that retailers are divided in one of two camps: those that don't know how to best achieve a strong ecommerce platform and those that are worried about its impact on the offline part of their business.

The Current World

We all know that one of the largest expenses for retailers, next to the cost of goods and payroll, is their cost of occupancy. In some situations, occupancy costs may even outstrip the other two costs combined. The biggest challenge faced by retailers is that these costs are not going to come down in the near future. As much as retailers may want to try to reduce or manage their occupancy costs, the advantage is always with the developer. Most certainly the occupancy costs in premium malls will never come down, and the cost of entry will remain high.

To compound the issue of occupancy costs, most developers at renewal time want stores remodeled and sometimes relocated in the centre. The financial impact of that capital expenditure belongs to the retailer. In addition to this, wage increases and the cost of inventory will continue to rise over time. The current 1-2% sales increases retailers are earning today is inadequate for some to keep up with operating costs, which therefore pushes more retailers into financial despair.

One interesting aspect of this evolution is that independent retail operators, with a strong vision and a savvy online ambition, have the opportunity to level the playing field in many retail categories. Even if they are local operators with a few stores, they can be formidable competitors with their virtual stores.

The Next Generation of Retailers

Even though retailers see the emergence of online retail, their activities to include it as a sales driver are minor. The shift in shopping will spur more online retailers in the next few years, cutting into and eroding offline sales and making it impossible to sustain a level of sales growth that meets growing costs. Therefore, the inflationary period of store expansion for many retailers is about to become a major liability.

In the US, Amazon is already closing in and making growth difficult for many. The best-in-class retailers will likely make some serious inroads into the online world. However, they need to understand how to embrace social networks equally as well before they can effectively make the leap.

As the cost of offline occupancy increases and retailers begin to look closer at their real estate portfolios, the number of profitable stores will shrink and there will be some very tough decisions in the next couple of years. Even retailers with successful brands who in the past would have leaped at every new store opportunity should question the financial viability of opening in some second-tier malls, and especially third-tier shopping centres. To remain competitive, retailers will have to go beyond just embracing e-commerce; they will need to create a virtual store that motivates consumers to visit the offline stores. The key to success will be making the complete service experience online and offline equally as captivating and satisfying.

The next generation of retailers will have fewer stores and an online platform that contributes significantly to sales and profits. The emergence of virtual stores that mimic their offline service will be critical for the overall experience and performance.

Service is another key component that the next generation of retailers needs to come to terms with. During the last two decades, retailers have been eroding service hours to make up costs, in many instances at the expense of customer satisfaction and retention. In fact, there is a generation of consumers that doesn't miss what it never had. Nevertheless, service and product choice will be two areas by which consumers will judge their overall retail experience as satisfactory, and a reason to return.

In the online and offline world product is a key driver, and this remains the largest opportunity to differentiate your brand from others. Price will remain a significant contributor to how quickly you can move product out the door. It is far wiser for retailers to have the correct pricing strategies in place rather than formulate one discount strategy after another.

As a retailer I have read and come across some interesting customer experiences with online shopping. The primary issue is one of returns to the offline stores when something doesn't fit or isn't what was ordered can be a little problematic for consumers and their perception of the retailers value proposition becomes negative. It can be a troublesome process to manage returns at your physical store however it shouldn't be impossible and yet it still happens.

Consumers will always presume that online retailers have the absolute best price with the discount factored in. However, while this isn't entirely correct, offline retailers that continuously offer discounts will have a more difficult time convincing online consumers that they are being offered the best price. As offline retailers decide how to formulate and strengthen their e-commerce strategies, online retailers will forge ahead at a fast pace.

Recently, a friend told me of an experience at a large electronics store chain. He wanted to buy a Tablet and was told that if he bought it on-line he could save $70. When he asked if could get the same offer in store, he was told no. All that effort to drive to the store and he was redirected to their on-line platform. None of this makes sense both from a customer service or retention perspective. And of course the perception about pricing on-line versus in store creates consumer distrust. As a result the electronics industry and others are worried about show-rooming. The truth is that show-rooming is not a phenomenon but a new part of shopping that can be taken advantage of if the retailer has the ability to provide these customers with added value they may even be able to close the sale.

In the final analysis the use of technology in stores and building a successful ecommerce model can no longer be ignored. Consumers have already begun to view the internet and social networks as a part of their regular life and retailers who are ignoring both through lack of knowledge or experience to do the right things are already vulnerable. The speed with which many companies move from a position of admiration to borderline extinction will grow even faster. Therefore, the importance of staying relevant in this new and evolving economy has never been more important.

Executive Notes: Keep Reaching for New Customers

- As the CEO and member of the board of directors, developing a competitive business model is one of your main strategic priorities.
- Increase the communication between real estate/business development and your marketing teams.
- Begin developing your virtual store strategies.
- Store design teams and your virtual store marketing team need have the same goals and objectives.
- Be prepared for the impact of fewer and or smaller stores and the cultural backlash it can have organizationally.
- Changing strategy to remain relevant and competitive is one thing; changing culture can destroy your brand.
- Does your organization have the nimbleness to divert its resources and energy swiftly? If not, change will take longer.
- How does your team need to evolve?
- Realistically, how much longer can your current business model survive and remain competitive?
- What is preventing you from growing a revenue generating online strategy?
- How do your retail operations need to improve in service?
- Do you have the organizational competencies and capabilities to execute and exploit a new direction?

Chapter 9: Customer Conversion – the Myths and Reality

Principal 9: What you need to know about conversion is that it is within your control. Whether you want more transactions per customer or more customers converted, all you have to do is train your retail sales team to deliver your processes the right way.

Not every business is like Apple where customers storm your stores to buy your products in anticipation of the next innovative announcement. Some fashion houses have this type of a following, but the rest of the retail world needs to fight for its share of the market. Most retailers could only hope to have this level of customer loyalty, and for that matter traffic and conversion.

Over two years ago, I began my own research on the best practices employed to improve conversion within retail organizations. Most of the practices I uncovered are not new, although there is consistency in the behaviour of the best-run retail organizations and a lack of it in the worst-run.

Let's begin this analysis with some of the myths about conversion, and then we will look deeper into the realities.

The Myths about Conversion

i. All consumers are price driven (they love discounts).

ii. Price matching strategies increase conversion.

iii. Most people are just browsing.

iv. You can judge customers by how they dress.

All consumers are price driven:

This is not true. Everyone places a value on products and services, and with that they equate a certain level of quality to each. Price is only what they are willing to pay for that perception. If your consumer model is heavily weighted into discounting, and whether your offers are advertised or not as a retailer you have made price the issue. This is usually the case where products are commoditized and a retailer cannot find ways to differentiate their brand with services.

Price matching strategies increase conversion:

Not only is this a useless exercise, it makes it open season on your brand to be regarded as overpriced. The right pricing strategies are those that match the brand's value proposition. Matching competitive prices is an interesting tactic (not a strategy) to convince consumers you will not be undersold. However, what it also says to suspicious consumers is that you knew you may be overpriced.

Most people are just browsing:

There is plenty of research that demonstrates quite the opposite. Certainly, a consumer may be waiting for the opportunity to buy (e.g. payday), but the intent is there. Most retailers do not train their staff well enough to engage customers and improve conversion. You will note in the next few pages that browsers are a significant opportunity for growth. Many of these browsers are quiet buyers or introverts who do not want to be served the same way as extroverts.

You can judge customers by how they dress:

A few years ago I had a retail employee tell me that a male customer who had just walked in holding an infant could not afford to buy beyond a certain price range because he had family obligations. After trying to convince the sales clerk otherwise, I engaged the customer myself, and guess what? He was a surgeon on his day off who ultimately bought luxury product.

The Realities about Conversion

Retail organizations with poor operational execution and even less support in training allow myths to cultivate. Myths are a multitude of excuses given to weaknesses in operational standards and execution of sales procedures. Ultimately, excuses take on a life of their own.

Generally, most retailers define customer conversion as the number of consumers who have visited their stores and bought. I always asked the question, why isn't conversion 25%, 50%, or even 100%? Where do retailers go wrong with their efforts to build conversion?

I have witnessed some farfetched calculations on conversion, including subtracting abstract anomalies to prove lower real customer traffic numbers, in an effort to improve the overall conversion number and justify low performance. Instead, every CEO and CMO should insist that the raw number is on the table as a measure of how many footsteps were brought into the store. Then a healthy discussion should ensue as to why everyone didn't buy.

What Helps Conversion at the Store Level?

For the most part strong branding, having bought and or designed the right product, and the right pricing strategies and merchandising practices help conversion at the store level. In addition, the store's general layout also helps conversion, allowing consumers to browse and eventually buy something with a retail staff properly engaging browsers. So why isn't that usually enough to grow conversion? What we forget is that during peak traffic days and periods, staffing properly and staffing for higher productivity with the right sales people will make a significant difference to your sales.

My research shows that four key aspects to driving conversion need to be executed flawlessly, though they rarely are:

i. Scheduling to traffic patterns daily and hourly
ii. Adhering properly to service operating procedures
iii. Engaging browsers
iv. Staff training

Scheduling – First, let's review what happens in an environment with inconsistent staffing practices. It leads to poor service, resulting in low sales and lower incentive payouts, followed by poor morale, which creates another ailment within retail: high turnover. Companies and their managers often blame competition with aggressive offers for their drop in sales and luring their best employees away with higher wages, both propagating poor sales results.

That isn't entirely correct. Employees quit for many reasons: poor work environments, poor customer service, unsuccessful incentive programs, lack of career opportunities, and insufficient on-the-job training. All of these create missed opportunities to grow sales and the profit performance for the retailer, not to mention how much employee turnover costs retailers in lost productivity and profit. If you want to improve scheduling you must improve the cause for your retention issues and then turn your brand into a workplace of choice for casual and part-time employees.

Operating Procedures – The signs that a retailer is struggling with strategy and execution include:

- An array of offers at the door
- Window displays missing their marketable opportunity
- Far too many messages in the store
- Strategic errors with product and pricing
- Confusion of retail sales staff as a result of mixed messages and changes in operational direction
- Inconsistent execution of roles at the operations field level

As stated earlier, product and pricing are important factors with in-store conversion. There is no doubt that product drives sales, however when product is incorrectly priced or the designers and buyers were wrong in their selection, your only conversion tool will unfortunately become discounting or a liquidator. No service strategy can be delivered when operating procedures cannot be adhered to. Retailing is both an art and a discipline at the same time and it requires a different skill sets to improve performance.

Browsers – Browsers are buyers, so don't dismiss them! The difference is that they have yet to make the decision of where to buy. They are already in the marketplace, however sales associates usually steer away when they hear "I'm just looking" and that stops a sale from occurring. Browsers can be converted into buyers provided they are engaged in a familiar manner where they don't feel bullied or coerced into buying something. This is an opportunity to build relationships and make someone who is more private feel comfortable in your store environment. Engaging customers with an introduction to store services and products offered is usually enough to begin the dialogue (but not close the sale). Once browsers feel comfortable, they will decide if what you have just presented is enough to continue with a possible relationship with your store.

When these customers walk out of your store, you should be concerned. Were they engaged by your sales staff? Did sales staff try to make a personal connection, or simply follow their own routine when they heard, "I'm just looking?" Browsers can become buyers, provided they hear more about why it was a good choice to come in and consider buying from you. For example:

- Am I at the right place for my needs?
- Is there someone here that I can deal with?
- How can I trust that you are selling me the very best or latest?
- Are you an advocate of these products and services?
- Why I should buy from your store?
- Make subtle introductions.
- Don't be aggressive.
- Allow them to be in charge.
- Let them know you are there to serve them.
- Be friendly but do not close in on their shopping space.

Retailers could invest wisely in training their staff to handle both introverted and extroverted buyers. The introverts are generally most of the browsers.

Staff Training – Training is a commitment toward creating a sustainable brand position in the marketplace. The success of any training and development program is evidence that a well-trained team can deliver a higher level of performance. There should be a return on investment (ROI) tied to this objective, and executives need to see this as a long-term proposition.

Build your sales teams capabilities to serve browsers and set clear expectation about service standards. Sales teams can be trained to provide a total customer service experience, provided the retailer knows their target customer and the drivers that will satisfy their needs. Therefore, building professional in-house programs that drive the expected level of customer satisfaction and service is an imperative.

What is the difference between Luxury Brands, Successful Franchises and All other Retailers?

Two Examples: If you walk into a McDonalds, Tim Horton's or Starbucks the experience is something that is continuously measured for consistency and quality. These brands would never have reached their level of performance if they didn't do that. Now consider Luxury retailers such as Ferragamo, Armani and Louis Vuitton, why do they have such a premium and luxury position? Once again it is their commitment to quality, consistency in service and innovation in fashion designs.

None of these retailers are standing still waiting for someone to point the direction they lead it and interestingly you can't barter for a lower price. Their brands perform well and they have a committed customer base. All of this would not have been possible if they hadn't placed emphasis in training to deliver flawless execution.

Strategies to Grow Conversion

Defining a core set of activities that will improve sales and the customer service experience in the store is key to building conversion and sales. You must have the right standards and principles in place to grow conversion, such as:

- Selling tools
- Merchandising practices
- Operational execution
- Internal communication

- Sales and customer conversion goals
- Scheduling that focuses on traffic periods
- Rewards for individual productivity beyond the averages

"Did you find everything that you were looking for?"

Why we ask this question when the customer is paying for their items seems often very redundant to me. The opportunity to have determined a customer's needs was while they were shopping not when they are ready to leave. It is a nice question, but it is often too late.

Ultimately, the next wave to grow conversion will belong to the retailer that is also able to embrace technology in their store environments. The experience needs to be of such a 'WOW' factor that it strikes a balance between emotions and satisfaction. It should not be complicated or technically complex where it confuses or frustrates past customers. However, it must be enough of a change in shopping that the customer will want to do it again. Service and customer conversion at the end of the day are simply one and the same and for all the pressure that is placed on retail stores to deliver more sales, the same level of effort is not placed on developing the competencies and capabilities of the retail staff to deliver that objective effectively.

When a consumer walks into your store they are not a customer until they have bought and that objective to convince the consumer to buy lies with the retailer and no one else.

Executive Notes: Create More Customer Transactions

Each retailer has their own incentive and sales associate strategies, yet there are simple rules to make it effective and ensure greater success.

- Define and reward the right selling behaviours.
- Do not let service suffer.
- Fewer hours does not mean more productive sales by selling staff.
- Add higher incentives to offset the disincentive of fewer hours.
- Evaluate the selling tools used in store; are they effective or do you need to introduce new ones?
- How effective is your staff training?
- Embrace technology in store.
- Simplify and make the shopping experience worthwhile.
- If the average dollar of your transaction is higher than the industry average your service and ability to convert consumers must be better than the average in the industry. Otherwise this is another reason you cannot grow customer count.
- If you were to evaluate the skills of each retail associate, how many would rate as customer friendly?
- Where do gaps in customer interaction require improvement?

Chapter 10: The Right Consumer Model

Principle 10: When you deliver the right product at the right price in the right environment, it is easier to mitigate the efforts of competitors.

For the most part, retailers are not maximizing their true sales potentials. As a result, many embark on change strategies that are on loose tracks, with a poor foundation and ineffective leadership.

Change Strategies

The reinvention of a retail brand does not always work. For example, recent news has been about a US-based department store and their quest for a new pricing model that eliminates unnecessary discounting and couponing. Obviously all has not gone well, as sales are down by 20-30%, dividends have been cancelled for the balance of the year, and analysts expect things to get worse.

On the one hand, retailers continue to face the challenge of change, while on the other hand they need to remain relevant. When a model is working, perhaps it is more a quest to enhance versus to disrupt with dramatic changes. Most change strategies in retail fail because more emphasis is placed on the model and not enough on first resolving the endemic issues, such as price, product, and service. Price and product will always be at constant war with one another because you can have several retailers selling the same products at different prices. The consumer dictates value, not the retailer, therefore regardless of price, the retailer with the best service experience will win.

A few retailers have successfully created a demand for their products and can command a premium price with only moderate sales events. They have done so through a visionary founder or leader who recognized that to be effective at growing traffic, there is the need to embrace not just your customers, but your employees and stakeholders as well. The issue with most retailers is the unenviable path of constant sales events and in-store deal making. It doesn't matter if the consumer does not like the main offer at the front door. By walking a little further into your store, they may find another compelling offer or the sales staff will work something out. This is the most destructive path retailers can take; unfortunately, it happens a lot, especially with retailers who sell comparable products.

Types of Retailers

The obvious questions to ask are: When is it the right time to change your consumer model? How do you do that effectively? Retailers fall into one of four categories as a result of their strategic choices and how they apply in the management of their consumer models:

Focused: For these retailers, price and product are equally matched with their service model. Their customers appreciate the value created, and as a result the retailers gain a strong loyalty and are able to build traffic and sales volumes and, equally important, cultural stability. There is a level of trust that occurs with this type of retail model and the customers who shop them.

Entrepreneurs: These retailers are more of an adventurer and are willing to embrace the right opportunities and pursue them. They launch new brands, products and models to test and try with consumers. Internally, they constantly look for the next breakaway strategy that will separate and identify them as leaders in the category. Their pricing strategies are stable and while they do have promotional sales, consumers recognize that they are getting a good deal.

Migrators: These retailers are always shifting from one consumer strategy to another and it is very difficult for them to pin down who they are and what they stand for. Consumers view them as the place to go to for a deal and it will be difficult to break away from that stigma once they have been labelled. Their cultural shifting is detrimental to any thoughts of longevity. When they attempt go dry and run equity type advertising, the decline in sales tends to be too high a trade-off.

Followers: As a retailer group they are simply copying the consumer model of the leader or the segment that they are in. They have not been able to differentiate themselves from other competitors and it is likely that they are in a commoditized segment of retail. To breakaway they would need to create a new model that offers uniqueness and a complete shopping experience, in addition to creating a pricing strategy that is relevant and competitive.

Retailers have to decide where they are within these categories. It is not always easy to accept your own reality and get on the path of change. The issue with launching a new consumer model and whether or not it will work is simply a question of how effective your organization is at managing change.

Managing Change

Changing your consumer model is somewhat of an undertaking that cannot be taken lightly. And to be clear it isn't just about setting new prices, it is about resetting your brand to become more appealing to the same customer base, a new one or both. And in that consideration resetting the brand requires a holistic approach that includes strategies, culture, people, training and commitment to delivering every aspect to a new model flawlessly. As mentioned in the executive notes, your ability to deliver the right outcome is contingent to the having the right people on this change initiative. Success may require introducing people who have the least involvement or sentiment to the brands past consumer model.

In all of the cases where a retailer has failed, or nearly failed, it is because change has been mismanaged. It begins with missing the right big opportunities and then scrambling to rewrite the consumer model. The process of change fails from the beginning when your tactics alienate your employees, then the consumers and last the financial markets.

Organizations that recognize the need to change sometimes tackle a cultural change first and still fail to achieve dramatic improvements. Unfortunately, they fail because they have gone too far with changing people instead of simply injecting new life into their consumer model. The second mistake made in launching consumer models is their lack of proper testing and rushing to re-launch an entire brand.

Executive Notes: When your Business Model isn't working

A consumer model is successful only when every aspect of the 4 P's are aligned and make sense to the consumer. Most lose their way on this and recovery is seldom easy.

- Do not copy another competitor's retail model, you will waste resources and valuable positioning.
- Ensure that you understand your customer base completely and the risks associated with making any changes.
- Test in remote markets and learn as much as you can about what works and does not work.
- Place your best people on this task and no one with any biases.
- Don't announce your new model internally until you have proven it.
- The biggest challenge is convincing the entire organization that this is important and must have the right resources behind it.

Chapter 11: When is Change Needed?

PRINCIPLE 11: WHEN IT COMES to change management, the trick is to know when, how, and who should lead it.

The difference between leaders in a retail category that are dedicated to the long-term growth and well-being of their organization versus those that are short-term, is simply one of paying attention to all the details. The details can be overwhelming, however when the profit and loss statement is your only report card, then you are missing all the early warning signals. Good retailers will take those early warning signals and begin planning and testing new initiatives (product, pricing, and services), gradually transforming their retail business in the right direction, bypassing the need for major and radical changes.

The rest scramble to catch up and institute (copying) what the leaders in their segment of the category are already doing.

Most times we jump into change when it is too late to make a difference. As I have noted in a few parts of this book, sales are usually the first barometer we use to identify that something is happening. However, in my opinion, the question of when to change is determined by constant monitoring and measuring progress. Management is always looking for that one blip that shows up on key performance indicators, and they are not always identified by a dollar sign.

The First Signs of Change

If there were such a thing as an early warning system, I believe it begins with inventory turnover and feedback from your stores. When marketing isn't delivering higher traffic and inventory isn't moving, particularly new products, the stores have a pretty good idea as to why. Being unaware of these issues is always a path to failure. The second opportunity for change is recognizing social, political, economic and technical changes. This is something that should be a focus of your enterprise risk management priorities.

The best retail executives can do is to create an early warning system that helps their team determine whether it's time for change and if overreacting is appropriate. The use of a regular GAP analysis or Balanced Score Card is the right course of action. The ultimate situation is an organization on a path of continually improving itself, its processes, its customers' experiences and ultimately its profitability.

The most effective position for a retailer to be in is one of continual innovation and testing of their current business model. Without such a culture of challenge and measures, there will be no change. A retailer that continues to rehash old ideas and resurrect some of them from the files of failed ideas should not consider itself as an innovator. Innovation for executives running retail organizations should mean:

1. Not being risk adverse
2. Being willing to reinvent yourself
3. Continuously improving customer experience
4. Leading and creating trends
5. Rewarding those who bring ideas forward

Innovation requires strong leadership and a board of directors that continuously asks the following questions: Are we still relevant? How much time does our current position still have in the marketplace? Are we able to change and pursue the right opportunities? Are we capable of identifying and implementing the right strategies? The greatest risk retailers face is not asking the difficult questions and challenging their organization in a way to remain relevant.

How many failed companies didn't see change in their segment of the industry as a threat? I wonder what the management and the boards of Circuit City, Borders Book Stores, and Blockbuster, to name a few, would have done differently to offset the changes they faced in the marketplace?

In my opinion, these and other companies needed to have greater dialogue with management about strategies and choices.

Whether you are trying to revitalize your existing business model or replace the one you have the key factors driving success is the ability to manage change effectively. What is of absolute importance in replacing your old consumer model is not to have the same team that has been working on the old one as the leaders behind the new one. Obviously the tendency for biases and lobbying for similarities to operational practices can and will build road blocks not always assuring a brand can make a smooth transition. Another important aspect is to understand the outcome you want. It is simple to say more traffic and transactions however, what will be different about the new consumer model that will attract more consumers into buyers? Is it pricing, product, service, merchandising practices, advertising, or moving into a less competitive segment of the market? Changes such as these require a strong level of testing and openness to new ideas to deliver a stronger consumer model. Ultimately, the success of any change strategy requires a great deal of consumer feedback that will support most of your initiatives. The lack of testing and consumer research drives the probability of success lower when it is driven by an individual or group's vision and ideas alone.

Many retailers fall short of their objective by either changing their consumer model too fast before they have worked out all the bugs or too little for the consumer to recognize an appreciable difference in any aspect of the model. At the core of all the barriers is fear that the financials may be impacted. However, if your retail business is already losing money then it may be so far past a recoverable stage that the resources to turn it around pose the same risk as trying to run it in its current state. Inevitably if you want to change the current performance of your business a leader must set the stage and begin by allowing others to let go of the old consumer model.

Keep in mind that the right time to question your position in the market is every day that you lead as an executive or oversee management as a director on a corporate board.

Executive Notes: Knowing how, is just as Important

Pursuing change strategies without an effective plan, resources and advocates is a recipe for failure.

- If your business culture is not predicated on managing change effectively, think twice before you leap. The road to change can be a difficult one.
- Build a high level of focus on the importance of making this successful.
- Know who to trust and who you will need to manage through this process.
- Constantly update on progress and ensure transparency.
- Don't lead the process alone involve your leadership team to take a role.
- Be mindful that your strategies can fail for one of two reasons: the strategy is wrong or the organization doesn't have the right competencies and capabilities within its functions.
- If the corporate board recognizes the need for change, it should begin with an evaluation of leadership.
- If a new leader is recruited, the board should be very involved in the formulation and direction of strategy.

Priority III: Leading Change - Chart the Course

Chapter 12: Leadership

Principle 12: Not all leaders are able to manage change. Past success in one organization is not a predictor of future success, nor that it is right for the culture.

It could be argued that the difference between a winning and an underperforming business in a marketplace where they occupy the same space is simply sales and profit performance. While that is one measure, it is not the reason you win. With that said, leadership plays a big part in delivering the level of results required. It's the type of leadership that works or fails in any business that CEOs and boards need to watch for.

In this chapter I deal with two subjects: operational leadership (how to best lead the front lines for the best results) and executive leadership (the type of leader for your current business situation).

Ensuring Operational Consistency

Organizations that respect the importance of flawless execution may last longer than those that fear implementing operational discipline. By discipline I am referring to the type of operational leadership where processes and experiences that customers encounter have procedures and customer-centric activities that can be measured. In retail, few organizations adopt a system where the quality of a service experience is measured. Most retailers refrain from using it because it is so process driven, yet within the QSR (quick service restaurant) industry it creates consistency and operational focus.

Many field managers and their organizations recognize the value and importance of store level observation and feedback systems to improve performance. Unfortunately, not all retailers are the same and there is a great deal of inconsistency with the execution of a customer's service experience.

Retailers can have a great number of procedures in place, but without an effective program, organizational consistency will not exist. Without the right systems and programs, there are many operational differences within a retail brand. When a market has poor results, quite often the local economy or competitive forces are blamed and marketers and merchandisers may be sent to the field looking for competitive differences. However, the truth is you should always begin with operational execution. When that is amiss, there is no point attempting any kind of strategic changes. In addition, retail executives often target underperforming field managers and manage them out of the company when there are poor results. While we all need to continue to improve the calibre of people on the team, without effective and approved field/store evaluations and processes, a new team member will be no further ahead.

How to Evaluate Service

Generally, a properly thought-out service evaluation includes the following:

1. Service
2. Merchandising practices
3. Store promotional visuals
4. Front door and window displays
5. Cleanliness
6. Lighting
7. Scheduling
8. Training

These evaluations need to have scores and be tracked as a part of the field manager's performance. Effective field managers are proactive and do not react to business conditions. They know their best and worst stores, know where the opportunities lie, and have a plan in place for each. They proactively engage their teams to focus on winning every day. In addition, these evaluations should provide other functions with insights into the organization's risks and opportunities. Operational evaluations and execution of the same is a top-down initiative that aligns strategies with in-store service expectations. Without the proper systems in place, your retail business will fall into a trap of collecting field feedback that is anecdotal at best.

The Operations Leader

This role usually has the title of Director or VP of Operations. As a member of the team that reports to either the COO or CEO, this person needs to be very effective in the role. As leaders within the retail organization, they are accountable for ensuring flawless execution of corporate strategies at the field level.

Numerous types of leadership styles will either make or break your business. Much depends on the style of leadership that is brought into the organization, and this is especially true of those responsible for the operations of your front-line field and store managers.

Operational Leadership Styles that Do Not Work

I will outline four leadership styles that do not work for the front lines of your retail operations. I believe that retailers hire too often for the wrong reasons. I have worked with each of these styles of behavioural characteristics in each business that I have run, however I took extreme precautions never to promote or hire someone with these behaviours.

The Controller – These individuals portray themselves as experts in whipping your operations teams into shape with regimented best practices and tools. The unfortunate part is that they are distant from a relationship standpoint and are not good at orchestrating effective programs operationally. While they can bring a great deal of order and structure because of a stern personality, they can easily alienate your teams, casting doubt about the cultural direction of the company. You can identify this style by the feedback you receive from your operations teams. These leaders portray themselves as in charge of more than they are really responsible for, and claim to have influence or be tight with upper management. There is a significant tendency to deflect responsibility for poor results on everyone and usually escape being disciplined for the same. The risk with this leadership style is that if unchecked, they will continue to operate under the premise of invoking fear to entice change and results. Promoting or hiring this type of individual to a lead operations role or a higher senior position can be detrimental to morale and the culture of the organization.

The Comedian – This leadership style lacks substance. Much of their character is about being perceived as likeable and an approachable person to work with. These managers base their ability to improve performance on the personal relationships that they hope to cultivate with everyone at different levels. Regrettably, you can usually spot this style by their inability to make the necessary people changes; everyone is a "good guy." In addition, although many are promotable on their teams, few have had the necessary developmental investment. Expect little by way of analysis from these leaders. Instead, feedback and answers to senior management are not well thought out. They are also unable to execute strategies effectively and a great deal of their persona is easily damaged by conflict and confrontation.

Sports Commentator – With crisp analysis, these leaders try to bring out the best in their team. The number crunching and ranking of stores and people numbs the sports team into submission. The numbers seem to take precedent every day, yet there is little acknowledgement of individuals during the week or month. My main concern about this type of leadership style stems around execution: drilling down to how a team or individual achieved their results and discussions on how everyone else can get the same results is loosely achieved. Unaware, these leaders inadvertently dismiss those less interested in sport analogies as 'not team players,' and in their mind this is the reason for that employee's lack of performance. In addition, don't look to this style of leader to deliver long-term results. Their demeanour is for short-term wins and they will usually not be able to cope with keeping stride with strategic direction.

Political Activist – Always huddling with upper management and portraying themselves as having the inside scoop and ear of the CEO. They promise promotions and increase the responsibilities of those they need on their side, reminding everyone that they are in a good place career wise. When results are not achieved, they tighten the reins and provide an oratory at weekly meetings on what they believe went wrong and how they are working closer with different functions to make up the shortfalls. They tend to be quick with the answers and equally fast at deflecting responsibility. This type of leader while strong in their communication skills is too wrapped up in the political aspects of their role to lead people and resources.

All four leadership styles are difficult for a team or individual to follow with trust and ensuring along the way the right level of communication, operational execution and delivery of effective results. Senior management the CEO or their executive responsible for that brand needs to address the lack of effective leadership in their organization.

Operational Leadership Styles that Work

Leaders in this role need to have a high level of business maturity or they will not be able to lead effectively. The best leadership style is one that demonstrates the following competencies:

1. Ability to stand alone as a leader
2. Coaching and development
3. Results orientation
4. Team building
5. Operational execution
6. Recruitment and selection
7. Focused on business improvement

Ultimately your operations leader is able to articulate corporate strategy into a working plan that is easy to deliver and engages retail operations and other functions to ensure thorough execution.

Generally I advocate for hiring the right search firm to conduct your recruitment. However, if an organization is committed to promoting from within, then the best scenario is to develop these skills internally so that they culturally fit with your short – and long-term business needs.

Executive Leadership

Few roles require as much discipline as the president and chief executive officer. A lot also depends on the structure and reporting of the retail organization. Is it a Canadian operation with its own infrastructure or a foreign retail operation where the Canadian office is a satellite operations team with some functional support? Having spent time overseas and speaking with other retail executives working outside of their home country, I learned that many have or wished they had more autonomy. There is a considerable difference in performance and culture when an organization can operate with its own leader and structure. Hence appointing the right person to lead your business locally or abroad is equally important and if you are not getting the results, it may be the culture that's in trouble. Many local and international roles are filled with competent people, however sometimes unrealistic expectations from a board or corporate can derail the best of plans and good executives.

I often relate a new leader taking over a business as analogous to what may happen when an insensitive or inconsiderate step-parent moves into a family's home. Initially when moving in, the focus may be on getting along with everyone in the household. After a few months, the new stepparent may begin to instill his/her personal touches on discipline and order. After a few more months, the biological parent may notice that family values and traditions are being changed, the children seem frustrated and quiet and are no longer talkative at the dinner table, not feeling comfortable in their home. The stepparent may continue to assure the biological parent that the kids are just adjusting and things will be fine. After a while, new duties and rules may be communicated, expectations are high and unrealistic and the kids may think back that, "Our mom/dad would never have allowed us to be treated in this way." One by one, the children head off to university or to look for work. What used to be a warm, caring family has been disrupted by someone who may have felt the family's values were in need of change or were unimportant to them.

Perhaps this is too severe an analogy for a company with a new leader, however the emotions and heartbreak are always the same. There is an element of failure in many organizations that promote or hire a new organizational leader (CEO or otherwise) who is not a good fit. I am not convinced that any board should allow one CEO or president to create cultural havoc and take apart the fabric that made a brand successful. Often boards that are desperate for a change in business results are looking for a white knight who can turn the business around.

I have heard board members say that it is not their role to be operational. I argue that in a company that faces financial ruin or extinction, as a non-executive and independent director on a board, you have every responsibility to ask questions and challenge the CEO's activities against agreed-upon objectives and strategies. Most retail organizations that face failure or challenging times are in need of a leader who will be forthright with the issues at hand and what needs to change. Whenever that leader begins with threats or stoops to practices to pressure people out of the organization, the leader is quickly destroying a retail brand's culture. While the leader may be able to instill some financial improvements with the changes made, it will be short-term as the effects of these changes will soon begin to impact loyal customers. Usually the new CEO will exit the company within 2 to 3 years as his/her strategies begin to backfire, unless they move to preserve the momentum in their career.

In the corporate world new CEOs often come in and clean house, hiring their own from a past life in hopes of building a stronger organization. They then tell the board that performance improvements may not happen as soon as they had hoped as they and the new team need to unravel all the bad work from the last decade.

The Ideal CEO

What type of CEO is best for a retail company that either needs to turn around its performance and or revitalize a brand? In an ideal situation, it must be someone who will not do all of the above. A leader should be sensitive to the importance of the legacy and culture of a brand, manage any process of change with surgical precision, and focus on agreed-upon performance measures and the company's position in the marketplace with the board or owners, all along demonstrating respect for the people who built the company. When companies (not just retailers) struggle with achieving their objectives some organizations go down a path of making radical changes and not all of these changes are necessary. In addition the real challenge for leadership is determine the real cause for the failure of strategies and simply while we know that it is execution, it is not always the people that are at fault for that shortfall.

At the end of the day there are no white knights, just leaders who want to make a difference by embracing a company's culture and engaging its participants on a new level. That is not to say that there should be no personnel changes, only that they be handled properly. In a society where being socially responsible is and will continue to become more important to a retail corporation, you cannot ignore the importance of having the right leader for the right situation on board.

One of the many challenges faced by any organization is the quality of leadership they need to recruit and develop. Is it one that does the will of the company or someone that has the will to make a difference? Each type of leadership style has different aspects to their DNA that can deliver results provided it is the right type of environment and of course each has its benefits and opportunities. Where one organization calls for more of administrative traffic controller providing guidance the others may require an innovator and builder to define and pursue opportunities. Placing the right leader in a retail brand that is going through a cycle that requires specific leadership skills is as critical as defining the right strategies to pursue.

Ultimately the right leader should have the abilities to build a retail brand with the same level of detail provided in a luxury brand, regardless of their price, product, and service proposition. When a leader can supervise such a visionary transformation and engage an entire organization in the right direction it is much easier to achieve your overall brand objectives.

A Chief Executive's role for the most part within the retail industry has a shorter lifespan. The main challenge boards and founders of retail companies are facing is the threats and opportunities that are being created by disruptive changes in the industry. Because of this, changing leadership at the top at a healthy moment in a company's performance is not a terrible decision provided that the change in leadership moves the organization to the next level of being competitively capable. And as an addendum to this statement it is not resolved with someone who is younger or with an ecommerce background. This is about having a leader with the vision and competencies to move an organizations culture forward. Not as easy a task.

Executive Notes: The Right Leader for the Right Role

Nothing is more important than an effective leader who knows how to move resources and influence the right outcomes. Experience is one trait the other is finding someone courageous enough to take on the job.

- Hire and promote to improve the organization.
- A leader should be someone who understands the importance of culture and can enhance it.
- Establish the necessary performance expectations up front with all C level executives.
- Don't hire a leader who has a caretaker attitude, especially when you want an organization to change.

Chapter 13: A Stress Test for Retailers

Principle 13: Never deny the facts or allow anyone to distort what the facts are telling you.

In what could be a continued stagnant market for the foreseeable future, retailers will fight harder for customers and talent to remain competitive. We are not in the same market dynamics as we were a decade or even five years ago. Over the last four years, banks around the world have undergone a financial stress test, with either a passing or failing grade. I think for those that passed and are responsible, they are better off and more aware of their issues.

Why do retailers need a stress test? Simply put, many of them are battling a change in everything from competitors, the way consumers shop and economics, all of which are playing on the health of a retail business. Retailers around the world are asking the question: how do you survive in a volatile market? Even international expansion for many has not yielded fast improvements in performance with a continued reliance on the home country business usually the USA or a European country to make up the shortfall.

For the first quarter of 2012, the UK reported that the number of retail bankruptcies increased 15% from the previous year. With retail sales around the world at a stagnant increase of .3% to .8% year over year, it begs the question: how many retailers are below that fault line? On an annual basis, approximately 14% of all business bankruptcies are from the retail trade. Unfortunately, the downward trend for most of these retailers begins with poor strategic choices in product, marketing, service, and overexpansion.

Components of a Stress Test

I believe that the majority of failures are preventable. It comes down to getting ahead of your business' issues before it is too late. The only way to do that is by developing and implementing your own stress test. A stress test for retailers should evaluate several key performance measures, beginning with competitive endurance, consumer relevance, service differentiation, innovation, brand appeal, strategic flexibility, growth strategies, ability to execute strategy, and financial performance. These key measures are by no means appropriate for all retailers, however they do force retailers to think further about how strategies are developed and executed.

Competitive Endurance – Are you chasing or leading the segment you serve? Have you secured a piece of the market that you can confidently call your own? Is your share of the market loyal or splintered? Is it driven by the next sales event? Do you and your management team know your position in the market and is it secure? Who else serves in your segment and are there competitors you can take share from? Does your sales volume decline when a competitor runs a sale? Are efforts to counter a competitor's promotional activities limited in changing your performance? This is not an effortless exercise and not unlike going down the path of assessing enterprise risk, this process will also require the same diligence and involvement of intellectual capital and facts.

Consumer Relevance – Are you changing fast enough in the marketplace and keeping up with consumer trends? Are your product buying choices, store designs, and merchandising practices creating an environment that drives traffic? Is your customer count and traffic increasing? Are you making up sales by taking price increases? Has your traffic declined at a faster pace than your ability to grow conversion and the average sale per customer? Mistakes in assessing this area are common because so much is subjective versus market driven data and you will need that and a little bit of vision to understand what your choices are.

Service Differentiation – Is your customer experience unique enough to differentiate you from our closest competitive rivals? Service is not something that you can fake. Have your employees bought in to the service strategy and company mission? If not, are relationship issues between you and your employees getting in the way of meeting customer needs? Can you count on your service practices to be delivered consistently? Are you able to implement new selling tools into the service experience with positive results? Can you describe your customers experience as consistent or a variable open to the attitudes and behaviours of a sales associate? There should be no doubt in a leaders mind that service is a key component to closing a sale, repeat customer purchases and overall loyalty. This is an investment in understanding your target customer.

Innovation – Are you pursuing technological advancements fast enough to be there when the consumer searches online for product and pricing offers? Are you encouraging an open forum on how to improve in-store service and product lines? There is a certain element of entrepreneurship that goes with being an innovator, and making the grade is determined by the consumer. Apple stores can attest to that; they drive innovation and consumers are waiting for their next generation of products. It doesn't matter if you are in the apparel, appliances, or automotive side of retail, the leader will be an innovator in customer experience and product offerings. A leader must always ask themselves are we perceived as a place where you will find fashionable new trends, product innovation and services that are appealing? If the answer is no then the journey must start here.

Brand Appeal – Experience has shown that retailers who pay particular attention to their front door with professionally-done visuals and the right level of messaging draw more traffic. Once in the store, are those browsers seeing what you promised in your advertising copy and front door messages? The look, feel, scent, and sound in your store create an appeal that should draw more traffic. That experience should leave a memorable imprint. I have always viewed the front door of a store as an open invitation to all consumers. It is a skill and an art to create the type of attractive invitation that will draw traffic. Many of the best retailers are leveraging sight, sound and scent to attract all the senses and set the mood for customers when in the store.

Strategic Flexibility – What is your ability to respond to environmental changes? How long will you stay with an unproductive strategic initiative? Do you have the internal ability to shift gears in strategy as needed? Is your management team evaluating and developing contingency plans to prevent derailing scenarios? Are your marketing strategies effective and paying out the ROI you are looking for? I have often heard that the strategy has been set and it isn't changing. However, when the sales are not coming in, there may be something wrong with the strategy or its execution. And it is usually this blind faith in decisions that destroys the long-term success of retail organizations. This is not to suggest that retailers change their strategies every week, however if it isn't working you need to react.

Growth Strategies— Do you have a plan in place that will drive your online revenue growth over the next 3-5 years and representing growth of 20% or more? If you are planning international expansion, do you have the financial facilities to ensure you reach your objectives? Are there extensions to your brand that will allow for further growth? Are you in a position to launch a new brand with fewer stores and a larger online presence? Growth cannot be in the hands of those within the organization that do not understand how to continue to challenge the current status of the business.

Operational Leadership (Execution) – How are you ensuring complete organizational execution? When it comes to execution, I believe too much is left to chance with the weekly updates and memos that come from the corporate office. Without consistency throughout the chain, it will affect customer perception of service and messaging. There are plenty of audit tools that have been developed to ensure operational compliance. If you fail to deliver consistency in your stores, it will affect your overall business strategy and financial performance. I am a strong proponent of detailed field visits, coupled with an appropriate level of evaluations and measures to ensure consistency. This process, backed up with a reporting of these visits, will help the organization to improve its support of store execution. Retailers need to make their operator's field teams not only responsible for execution; they also must be an equal partner in understanding the issues and what is expected. There are alarming differences in performance. I am referring to strong results with field managers who are engaged by senior management on strategy, financial performance, and competitive feedback. Organizations that allow a field team to operate blindly without relevant information are missing two opportunities: stronger financial results and the opportunity to develop their teams.

Financial Performance – Financials are an important measure, particularly around liquidity and stability. Emphasis on payroll should not be dismissed, although there is too much emphasis in troubled retail organizations regarding hours. I was in an electronics shop with my wife and she overheard a store manager say, "Start sending people home, we don't have the sales to keep everyone on." To begin with, consumers in the store don't need to know about your problems! Secondly, productivity should be managed differently by introducing store and individual sales staff key performance indicators (KPIs) as performance measures. Most retailers are reluctant to do this for two reasons: you have to invest in the development and rollout of a program that offers skills training in managing conflict and coaching; and there is a need to change retail culture from a passive, social one to a practical, performance-driven organization. Can you define in your weekly meetings which markets and stores are under-performing? Do you know which products are moving and can you replenish fast enough? Are you in a position to purchase fresh product and eliminate the negative impact of product that doesn't sell? Ultimately, are you financially troubleshooting or developing your business?

The Usefulness of a Retail Stress Test

It is easy to understand why a retailer can be reluctant to conduct a self-assessment of their brand; after all, nothing more can bring about greater scrutiny of management's ability to manage the four critical elements to remaining relevant. The ability to identify the right opportunities and objectives, craft supporting strategies, and demonstrated skills in their implementation and execution. The experience of many failed retailers was that they lacked insights and did not see competing threats which lead to supporting the wrong strategies. They also struggled with how to turn away from strategies that were not working.

In any period of time and under any business circumstances one of these invariably might go wrong. And often it seems when things are at their worst we forget these critical steps and their overall importance.

- Identifying the right opportunities or objectives
- Crafting the right supporting strategies
- Capabilities to implement strategies
- Competencies to execute effectively

The strength of a retail organization lies in their discipline to improve performance and stay relevant in a competitive market. However, when these four critical steps are even marginally weak performance will not being maximized.

Market driven retailers understand the importance of these four elements and the critical nature of their impact or lack of it if they are wrong. A stress test in any manner that you design it should be conducted by people in your organization that will not be moved by personal biases. As a leader you want to have the facts on where the opportunities exist and understand the elements that need to be employed to improve your current situation.

The bigger risk is not to be aware of your abilities to manage in difficult times. The stress test is not solely intended to determine your strategic thinking skills as much as it is to identify your organizations abilities to address internal and external risks and opportunities.

Use the following simple stress test to ask some tough questions about each key measure. A score of 1 is low and a 5 is high. Most retailers with underperforming brands may not feel it is necessary to go through such an exercise.

Sample Stress Test

		1	2	3	4	5
Competitve Endurance	- Are you able to sustain and grow your market share? - Is your share of voice effective? - Do you achieve traffic and conversion goals?	☐	☐	☐	☐	☐
Consumer Relevance	- Why do consumers shop your stores? - Can you define what needs to change to become/retain #1 or #2 in your category? - Have the last 5 years of sales growth been positive?	☐	☐	☐	☐	☐
Service Differentiation	- Is your service model unique? - Does it create a positive and memorable customer experience?	☐	☐	☐	☐	☐
Innovation	- Is technology leveraged as a capability for both the organization and consumers to improve rentention and the experience?	☐	☐	☐	☐	☐
Brand Appeal	- Are you setting trends or chasing them? - Are you buying for the brand experience or for the next possible sale?	☐	☐	☐	☐	☐
Strategic Flexibility	- Do you have the internal management capabilities and competencies to change course and define breakaway strategies?	☐	☐	☐	☐	☐
Operational Leadership	- Do your stores have a high level of operational execution and consistency? - Are your selling skills effective?	☐	☐	☐	☐	☐
Financial Performance	- Is the organization working against the right KPIs? - Does management at all levels understand the financial objectives? - Is inventory management at the top of your cost focus?	☐	☐	☐	☐	☐

Executive Notes: Stress Tests need to be Objective

A self-evaluation needs to begin with a team that has the desire to improve their short and long-term performance. The next step is for that team to have the internal fortitude to be honest with themselves and those that they report to.

- If your strategic effectiveness, retail operations, and financials were to be put to the stress test today, how would your business fare? Are you ready for a competitive intrusion or a new game-changing business model? Or will your brand be making all the waves?

- The board and the CEO should question every assumption and aptly differentiate personal biases from facts.

- It is important to remember that some members of a management team would look at these stress tests as a means to identify weak performers instead of opportunities to improve the brands position. When that occurs protectionist attitudes get in the way of making changes.

- Leadership teams must complete these internal assessments with feedback from key functional leaders who are closest to the opportunities.

- Always check your position in the market. Who is winning market share? Why and how?

- Stay on top of consumer preferences in service and product.

- If you must operate leaner in store, do it with technology to differentiate yourself from competitors. Speed of service is a key consumer driver.

- Mediocre products or unappealing fashion choices are not going to help your differentiation strategies.

- Execution, execution, execution – if you can't deliver it right the first time it will be your internal threat.

- Conduct your own stress test annually and before you plan next year.

Chapter 14: Competitive Endurance

Principle 14: Don't believe your own internal press about your position in the marketplace; consumers and competitors may think otherwise.

With the current global competitive landscape, even if you already enjoy a number 1 or 2 position in your category, it is likely at some point that you will be derailed by a new player with a more attractive business model. The flexibility to change is in the hands of the leader of the organization. Your organization's competitive readiness is something only the CEO can determine with the assistance of key members from their senior executive team. A lack of preparedness is something that will be visible in one of two situations: a market or country where a major retail brand has entered the marketplace, or you are noticing continued erosion in traffic and it becomes increasingly difficult to meet your financials.

In 2013, Target will launch their brand in Canada. Retail leaders around the world are watching with interest to see how much of an impact a launch of this scale will have on the share of other retailers. It is a major risk for Canadian retailers who are not in a position of strength and for the old guard trying to remain relevant in consumers' minds. The increased competitive activities of retailers under attack by Target will be aggressive to retain their share. At first a few smaller chains will begin to feel the effects of Target. For that matter other major retailers like Walmart, who will not sit it out, will also respond in kind to keep their share of the pie.

The speed and competence with which local and national competitors respond to a competitive threat such as the one in Canada will determine their ability to sustain their own market share and results. The most effective way to accomplish this goal is to have the right organization in place.

In such a situation, retailers have little time to waste and they will need to immediately assess their management teams in every function throughout their brand. An effective leadership team will be one that is both planning ahead and that is responsive to changes in an actively competitive market.

Competencies and Capabilities

To achieve your goals, conduct a total management team evaluation against the objectives you have set and the skill sets needed by your organization. The unfortunate part is that the competencies of key management are not always aligned with the objectives the organization needs to deliver. Leaders must continuously evaluate and challenge their internal position of strength.

As an executive, I feel very strongly about the roles and impact each of these functions must have in a retail company.

Human Resources

This function must lead in the spirit of the organization's growth plans. The ideal human resource leader has experience in several areas:

1. Developing a business culture
2. Change management
3. Training of front line employees
4. Succession planning at all levels, ensuring that your pipeline for talent never runs dry
5. Performance management and every aspect of performance, including coaching, counselling and annual reviews
6. Executive development
7. Employee relations
8. Compensation and benefits practices to keep your business competitive

Unfortunately, this function spends more time managing employee relations issues and approval of pay increases versus a sophisticated model for growth. The best-in-class organizations understand this and for them, human resources is a partner to both management and employees. There is a greater ROI when HR has a broader role versus just getting payroll and managing performance for less competent managers.

Marketing

In this competitive and unpredictable environment, a CEO looking for a marketing leader needs someone who is entrepreneurially driven and has the equivalent maturity of a tenured CMO. Marketing leaders cannot be timid and risk adverse, nor should they be so bureaucratic in their approach that it paralyzes progress. These individuals must be competent and charged with direction to define strategic choices for developing new and existing markets, and innovative enough to influence and create trends. These leaders should be focused on leveraging technology so they can simultaneously build your virtual channel and advance your customers' experiences in offline stores, enhancing the service level eroded over the years by severe reduction in productive hours.

Operations

Within this function it is important to have a retail executive who has strong financial, marketing, and leadership skills. Equally important in this role is to keep the field and executive leadership focused on the implementation and execution of strategies. Too often people in this function are involved in program development and decision making that is not relevant to their role. Therefore, their involvement on key projects should be kept to customer satisfaction and the delivery of service.

Finance

The ideal leader in this role is a well-rounded CFO with past retail experience in managing key financial aspects of the business, such as inventory and payroll, in addition to providing regular interval summaries of business performance. This role should be the gatekeeper for the CEO, pointing out where the opportunities and risks exist with current strategies and initiatives. The CFO should be questioning every strategy and tactic for its impact on delivering sales and protecting cost centers within the P&L. Please review chapter 15 to see how a CFO can lead in further advancing the financial performance of a retail company.

Organizational Communication

Every goal and strategy must have measures of responsibility that connect the entire organization. They need to be communicated effectively to the retail group as a means to develop consistency and focus. At executive meetings the senior team should always question all communications leaving a department and heading to the stores or within the administrative functions that are not aligned with goals and strategies.

This chapter only lightly touches on the quality of skilled executives required in a retail organization. However, the quality of the talent is what will determine your competitive endurance.

This is an opportune point in the book to remind ourselves that to build retail business that is both relevant in the market place it must also have relevant leadership.

Relevant Leadership- Relevant Brand is

- A retail business that is aligned Organizationally and Culturally
- The right people with the right behaviours to engage the organization
- Those who also have the right competencies and capabilities to support their needs

Organizational Alignment: Foundational and Functional

An Organization that is properly aligned has gone out of its way to define the foundational and functional needs of the business to achieve its overall goals.

Cultural Alignment: Values and Principles

To achieve cultural alignment both values and principles are made clear to everyone; with values defining who we are as a brand and principles being clear about how we will go about doing our work.

Executive Notes: To be Considered 'Competitive' you must be Leading and Gaining Share

- How much of your management team in all functions is truly focused on winning in the market place?
- Are you receiving and delivering breakaway strategies? Game Changers or a re-hash of last years promotion.
- Create a culture that has a high level of urgency to deliver results. The CEO sets the stage for this level of ownership, and it is most effective when collaboration and trust has been given to the assembled team.
- Without measurements such as a Balanced Score Card or simple GAP analysis that measure the key aspects of a total plan, a fiscal year can be quickly lost. To monitor your performance, you will require robust and focused KPIs that call out over – and underperformance in key areas of the business.
- The one major reason why organizations lose their competitive edge is that their employees lose their focus and interest. Too often "flavour of the month" comes up as the reason organizations lose sales, share and profits. The reason for it is that employees are not getting the message. It is senior management's role to deliver one message to everyone with consistency and in unity.
- Your level of communication will depend on your audience and how precise you need to be. In a weak organization, more frequent is an appropriate approach. In a strong organization with a complete level of confidence in execution, it may be quarterly.
- Leaders need to manage the message because it can and will be diluted by those with poor communication skills.
- Each function must have a strong leader with proven domestic and international experience. The main reason is for your brands growth and the potential of significant foreign competition.

Chapter 15: How Successful Retail Brands Win

PRINCIPLE 15: STAY RELEVANT AND stay in the game.

Do retailers have to follow the same path to economic failure as Hemingway did, "At first gradually and then suddenly"? Scores of retail businesses around the world fail or find themselves in bankruptcy protection from their creditors. The retail industry faces important dynamic changes, and they are not just limited to uncertain economic times. The competitive landscape for retailers will remain complex, and the next five years will reveal which retail brands are able to handle the changes that are picking up momentum.

To remain competitive, retail brands must be able to redefine their value to consumers throughout their life cycle. That means making the appropriate strategic choices along the way. The speed with which you respond to changes, driven by an opinion-sharing and fast-paced socially connected consumer, is as important as having the right merchandise in your store.

Unfortunately, most retail businesses respond to downward trends in sales as the first indicator that something is wrong, although it actually wasn't the first. At this stage, some scramble feverishly with sales discounts and offers, others upgrade their service model, a few change their consumer model and yet others invest in store designs, new product lines and advertising. On the other hand, others will go down a path of cost cutting and make no effort to grow sales. All of these actions done in a piecemeal or grouped fashion will not guarantee a gain in market position.

Market share is what you ultimately lose in retail. That fate can arrive very quickly as a result of many factors, most of which are under your control and based on the choices you make. When in a fight for survival, businesses are sometimes looking so desperately for an opportunity that they make the wrong choices. In this chapter, I outline a theory that the life cycle of most retail brands is based on their current strategies and how consumers likely perceive these brands.

Is Your Brand Relevant?

How many brands are really going to be around in 10, 15, 20 years after their conception? I find it fascinating, the number of retailers that encounter competitive obstacles early enough to mitigate their impact or seize them as an opportunity and yet they do not act. At annual strategic planning sessions a thorough environmental scan of the internal and external issues reveals the obvious. What were the first signs that online retailers are a competitive threat? When did foreign retailers enter your market? How soon did you realize that cross border shopping was an issue? When did your product or service become commoditized? When did you realize that traffic declines were not a temporary issue? When did discounting become your only marketing weapon? Too often these and other issues are staring right at a management team or a board of directors and the questions are not asked or the management team is not challenged.

In Denial

When the leadership of a brand does not recognize its own opportunities and threats it is usually the first sign of a potential decline in their market position. When any business for that matter begins to believe that its strategies are good for the long-term and that they do not need to create new products or services, it is a classic mistake of ego. When the internet first began with some online retailers (who failed as they didn't have the resources and capabilities to serve customers properly) the offline retailers dismissed the internet as a passing fad. Today, we all now know the future turned out to be something very different. A retailer of an apparel company once told me that their category is all about fashion and as long they lead with fashionable trends, they will never lose their market position. Regrettably, this retailer found themselves in receivership and recovered only to find themselves closing a few stores and become much less of a player in the market. Why? Simply market relevance was being decided by one or a small group of people, changing their focus might have meant a change in leadership, suppliers, buyers, designers – a complete remaking of the company. Facing that kind of change will bring about risks that some retailers cannot afford.

What is a Relevant Brand?

In my view a relevant brand is one that is current, providing their target customers with the products and services that are aligned with what they are looking for today. These brands command the consumer's attention in service, selection of products, quality engineering, fashion, and value. To sustain that position in the market requires a continued focus on what is changing and how to adapt to it. Unfortunately not every retailer is able to respond to that as well as some can. Two leading retailers jousting in the same category will not survive the competitive strife between them unless one can continuously improve its product and service offering. Yet some manage to stay alive driven by heavy discounting and a continuous reduction in costs, which affects the quality of merchandise they sell and the service they provide.

Staying current in the minds of consumers is also a very important task for the marketing team of every retailer. However, the dismal path of continued sales events does not build brand equity it instead sensitises the consumer to your promotional behaviours and eliminates the opportunity to build the value of the brand. Unplugging from the promotional steroid is something that has not been done successfully without a painful outcome. Staying relevant means bringing value to consumers by way of product and service innovation and fashion trends, without these, you will be unable to move from the promotional calendar you run your business by today.

Retailers often comment that it takes time to train consumers to a new consumer model. I for one believe that the current level of social media involvement by consumers is changing all of that. And hence why many retailers haven't determined their strategies as of yet. How do you train consumers who share opinions with one another about products, services and events effectively without offending and drawing their repute for your comments and direction? This is the biggest challenge marketers are facing and as such just hiring someone who knows their way around social networks will not be enough.

The Retail Life Cycle

You can place retailers into one of four categories to describe their life cycle. As shown in the graphic below, each of these categories represents a stage in the retailer's life cycle in terms of growth in the market place and relevance with consumers:

- High relevance and high growth
- High relevance and low growth
- High growth and low relevance
- Low growth and low relevance

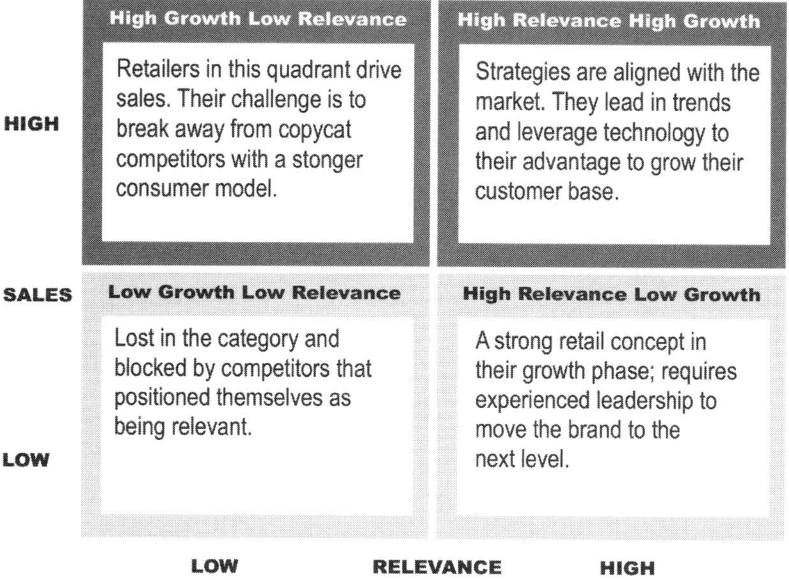

High Relevance and High Growth – This optimal level retail performer is clearly recognized by consumers as a leader and innovator in the category.

These brands are constantly searching to create or define the next trend. Usually these organizations focus on not just growth, but also on how to stay relevant in a fast-changing environment. They develop and introduce product lines and services that will continue to set them apart from their competitors. These retailers are operationally performance driven. Their culture is based on everyone knowing the goals and the tactics that will deliver their objectives. They score high on communication and senior management doesn't shut down feedback from the stores. They relish opportunities to improve service and execution. They have a high level of execution which includes defined service and sales practices that distinguish them from other retailers. The customer experience tends to be consistent and any shortfalls are quickly corrected. They likely spend appropriately to train their front line employees.

High Relevance and Low Growth – The highly relevant retail brand with low growth (not negative growth) may be at its start-up or rebuilding stage. This brand is likely struggling with not enough strengths and competencies in marketing, product, and merchandising practices. Consumers are attracted to their offering, but the retailer can't or chooses not to do enough of the right things to grow share. These organizations can score high on innovation and in building a strong retail brand. At a critical level, they may be missing the right target in their communication and selection of retail locations. A more experienced management team is needed for these retailers to reach the right target market and grow their business foundation. If in a rebuilding stage the CEO may still be working on the development of key functional competencies after years of stagnant performance and organizational biases that may have plagued thinking. In a start-up situation it could be possible that the founder, while a visionary, may not have the experience to move their organization to the next level.

High Growth and Low Relevance – These retailers are growing their top line with discounting, or may be at their milking stage if it has been a strong and recognized brand. They may be the leader in the category by volume, unfortunately they are unable to convince consumers of that. Therefore, they continue to drive sales with strong discounting. Loyalty is decreasing because of strong competitive offers. Retailers in this quadrant are easily exposed to new competitors and disruptive models. This type of organization needs to regroup and evaluate their brand's value proposition in the marketplace. It will be difficult for organizations such as this to sever themselves from price-driven offers. In addition, these retailers must convince consumers that there is a higher level of value in their product and services versus others in the same segment of the retail category. Most retailers that have lost relevance in this quadrant experience a higher level of competition. And since competitors have copied their model in product and service, there are no longer significant differentiators between them. To move from low to high relevance, retailers will require dramatic changes in the experience they provide their customers. They will need to be measurably significant in creating a compelling value proposition. A word of caution: what put most retailers in this quadrant is the pursuit of the wrong strategies. Discounting only creates what I refer to as the 'swarm': droves of consumers moving from retailer to retailer pursuing a compelling price or discount. That strategy does not create high relevance or loyalty. Investment in creating a new customer experience that includes technology not only enhances the experience but increase the time spent in the store. Many service related retailer could benefit from that approach.

Low Relevance and Low Growth – These retailers either didn't pay attention to the signals or were unable to identify them, believing it was just an economic situation that would pass and not a strategic one. Within this quadrant you will find many of the tired retail players who either have the opportunity to reinvent themselves and should, or those who have entered a stage where they have been pushed out of the segment that they have served and are either close to bankruptcy or have a small window to sell their business. Retailers in this quadrant who believe that they have an opportunity to reinvent themselves need to begin with a new vision of the future for the brand. They need to tackle every aspect of their organization. It now becomes a dissection of function by function and their ability to lead, execute and deliver their portion of strategies. It will require an evaluation of people and individual performance and making what is always a difficult call for change.

Most retailers will go through each of these quadrants in some point of their life cycle the question that they need to manage is do they know where they are today. Being relevant in the market is not something that is easy to achieve and certainly no vision statement alone will drive the necessary change. To stay relevant in today's environment will require paying close attention to each of these quadrants and conducting a stress test that will determine your ability to evolve and when to do it.

Change management can be very painful. However, with the right leadership, vision, and strategies it is possible for a brand to rebound and handle change effectively without cultural fallout. At one time, this was as easy as defining a customer profile: listing your customers' attributes and defining how you would attract, buy product, merchandise your stores, and serve them. Obviously, in this new world that will not be good or fast enough.

How do Winning Brands Stay Relevant?

The first word that comes to mind is discipline. The discipline of being tough on yourselves as leaders of the retail brand and asking the right questions about resources, marketing, advertising, product, the buyers, pricing strategies, operations, the quality of leadership, service, technology...to name a few. The discipline comes with the intent to not only be relevant externally but internally first and foremost. To stay relevant, winning brands make choices about their current position in the marketplace not once every five years at least twice a year.

Even if a brand leads in a category it cannot survive without continuous change and that change should always enhance the consumer's preference to shop from that brand. Achieving that objective assumes that you have spent a great deal of time studying your category and how it is evolving. And that requires relevant research information that some retailers are unable to conduct internally and need to do so with external resources.

The speed with which information is shared between consumers, their likes, dislikes and opinions, is of an unprecedented measure that has never been experienced before. In other words, bad news can travel even faster and reach a lot more people than ever who share in the opinion. Therefore, ignoring market research today is more of a risk than the cost itself and retailers who revel in doing it themselves with instinct and superficial research take all the risks. Retailers who want to be on the front end of trends and innovation need to with the right unbiased information that will assist them in sustaining their market position and changing as necessary along the way.

Winning retailers have built a discipline within their organization that is infatuated with the idea of a consumer that stays engaged with their brand. And with that comes a strong internal focus on protecting the brand from deteriorating in its position. All of this is impossible without strong leadership at the top and within each function, in addition to a strong level of internal entrepreneurial leadership.

A winning brand is able to magnify its position in the market place when it aligns the entire organization with a high level of communication and internal promotion of their goals and values. There is a difference in telling everyone what to do versus gaining everyone's commitment to achieve the objectives and values of the brand.

Simply, gone are the days where one leader could assimilate enough information to deliver a sustainable retail brand. Product and pricing alone are no longer the single drivers behind success, they may be able to drive sales short-term, however, long-term is more problematic in today's economy with a technologically and socially connected consumer. The best retailers will understand not to limit themselves to the old and embrace much more of what is new as with each generation of consumers the expectations will change. And as you consider this point, we should also reflect on the fact that those born after 1993, 'Generation Z', do not know a world without the internet and will likely view retailers that are below their level of technological understanding as redundant. In the final analysis, it may already be too late for some as they have succumbed to the very issues and opportunities pointed out here.

Executive Notes: Staying Relevant is an internal Discipline

In a complex world of change, retailers have one of two choices: lead change or chase it. The latter does not sustain relevance. I cannot emphasize enough the importance behind a team continuously looking for how to keep the brand alive and on at the top of a consumers mind in preference. So many organizations lose sight of this important internal initiative and once they slip to number two it becomes more difficult to prevent the brand from slipping to number three in awareness.

- *Innovation:* Is out in front of what's new within their category. They create trends and do not chase the others hoping to pick up remnants of their strategies.

- *Engaged Employees:* Being clear about what you stand for accomplishes three people goals – attract talent, retain talent, and then in turn that talent freely gives you all that they have to offer.

- *Operational Execution:* Time to market has never been more urgent and the ability to deliver accurately and flawlessly in service, operations, and communication with speed is a competitive advantage. This will require involving everyone in your organization. Organizations that have already embraced this value are making strong inroads to improve their current and future performance.

- *Technology Driven:* These retailers are fully invested in the use of technology to identify opportunities, craft strategies, engage employees, develop their teams, and grow sales.

- *Entrepreneurship:* The most exciting part of being a retailer today is that entrepreneurial skills are fundamental values within the organization and leaders need to create a culture in which talking about and taking risks is healthy.

Chapter 16: The "S Factor"

Principle 16: When it comes to growing sales, there is a method to success. However, the investment in time and resources must be consistent with the desire to grow sales, otherwise there are only limited results and missed opportunities.

In Chapter 9, you read about the challenges and efforts needed to convert your traffic into buying customers. It is not always an easy exercise to improve retail conversion. Depending on the retail segment you operate in, the traffic that is converted can be as low as 5–10%. I argue that while retailers can increase their sales through price increases and discounts, it is not a sustainable practice. Eventually you either run out of the ability to raise prices, or discounting becomes useless as a vehicle to drive sales.

The "S Factor" is something that you realize through years of experience in retail. However, very few have ever tried to characterize it in a manner where the value of your efforts is directed at delivering results. There is no natural formula that fits all. You will have to take your company and its leadership through an exercise to determine your ability to make the S Factor work for your brand.

The formula is:

S1 + S2 + S3 + S4 = Sustainable Growth
S1 = Service standards
S2 = Staff training
S3 = Store sales tools
S4 = Store experience

S1: Service Standards

You cannot begin to make changes and improve your sales unless you have clearly defined service standards for your brand. Ask yourself some of the following questions:

1. What are your defined operating procedures?
2. Who monitors them?
3. Are the service standards consistently applied in all your stores?
4. Does your field management team understand the importance of your brand's service standards and their role to uphold them?
5. Are these service standards integrated into all your initiatives?
6. Do these service standards go through an executive review for approval?
7. Is there a store assessment to assist you with delivering these service standards?
8. Is your sales staff comfortable with engaging customers at different points in their shopping experience?

S2: Staff Training

No level of service can be achieved without adhering to consistency and procedures. Ask these questions:

1. Is there a competent and expert training team in your organization that can effectively train and develop to change sales and service staff behaviours?
2. Does your organization have an effective on-board training program for new hires?
3. Are you clear about how training and coaching must be deployed at all levels within the retail organization?
4. Does your training program review effective product knowledge?

5. Is training as a function integrated into the implementation and execution of key programs and strategies?

6. Is this team effective at making advocates of your sales staff, of your culture, products and services? If not, what needs to change?

7. Are store managers effective at training and coaching?

8. Do the training efforts show up in an equitable manner, such as improved customer service and customer conversion? Are your loyalty and likely to return results higher?

S3: Store Sales Tools

Many stores have small change rooms for customers that are old and dusty and where boxes are sometimes stored nearby. The mirrors are smeared or chipped, and locks on the doors do not all work. Ask these questions:

1. Are your change rooms current, fresh, clean and appealing to allow customers to try on product?

2. Have you considered the use of technology so that customers can compare the apparel they try on without having to go back and try it on again?

3. Are your pricing strategies in store easy to understand?

4. Are there too many confusing markdowns or specially-marked products in the store?

5. Do you have an effective reward and incentive program in place?

6. Are your employees advocates of your product and services? Do they believe in your price value practices? Simply put, would they shop from you?

7. Can you simplify cashing out and eliminate long wait periods?

8. Is there an opportunity to engage customers with more product knowledge through the use of technology in the store?

S4: Store Experience

All the bells and whistles are meaningless if the store environment is not crisp and inviting. Your brand must attract and connect with all the senses. A customer walking by any of your locations must be able to say, "I know this brand" without having to look up at the store sign. For example:

1. Are store visuals are clean and damage free? Is the message appealing and does it magnify the brand's image?
2. Is the store staff engaging customers at all times?
3. Is the level of teamwork visible, and can customers sense a positive workplace?
4. Are sales staff appropriately dressed, either wearing brands or an approved uniform?
5. Does the use of technology simplify customer experience and the speed with which they are served?
6. Is the store staffed appropriately for both low and peak traffic periods?
7. Are returns and damaged merchandise issues handled with the same manner of respectful service as is a sale?
8. Are the in-store displays drawing customers to new product and identifying your brand as an innovator?

By managing aspects of the S Factor, the elements to grow retail brands go beyond sales alone. The S Factor contributes to four areas to enhance the performance of a retail brand:

1. Customer satisfaction and loyalty
2. Brand image
3. Value proposition
4. Market relevance

The diagram above shows how delivering the right level of resources ensures strong in-store execution, which is aligned with your overall strategies. This results in a much stronger ability to resist competitive threats and ensure continuity in the relationship you must deliver and maintain with your existing and new customers.

Customer Satisfaction and Loyalty

In my professional experience, training employees to deliver a unique brand experience that matches the attributes of the customer base you are targeting will only improve customer satisfaction and loyalty. In addition, within a franchise organization, it will take a little more convincing to employ new operating standards, especially if the retailer has not in the past held franchisees accountable for adherence to standards. One of the shortfalls of the training function is that training programs are not developed fast enough to keep up with the evolving service attributes customers are seeking in a store experience. If the store experience does not meet expectations, neither will customer satisfaction and loyalty.

Brand Image

Without standards of performance in place, a brand's image is whatever the employees want to make of it. When a brand allows dozens of field managers or 100 store managers to impress their own version of service upon their customers, the image of the brand is diluted by a variety of innocent mistakes. A strict set of service and operational standards must be in place for the right kind of execution.

Value Proposition

Defining the S Factor in your own retail strategy will ensure a greater sense of consistency in delivering value throughout the organization. It is crucial to ensure that the best practices are defined and continuously measured objectively. The executive leadership team needs to ensure that each step of the value proposition is protected from less experienced individuals who may want to impose their version of service.

Market Relevance

Remaining relevant in the marketplace will be a serious challenge for many retailers. However, creating a store experience needs to be based on tangible and measurable procedures. The elements created to make your brand unique are also creating consistency throughout the customer's experience. Ultimately, the investment on how to deliver training, whether it is one-on-one or through technology, should be measured by how well it improves the execution of service and the results delivered. Service is something that cannot be faked. Your organization either believes what you have to offer creates value for your customers or it does not.

In my career, I have interviewed many retailers at different levels of responsibility who are anxious to leave their current organization, and it is usually for one of two reasons: the S Factor does not exist, or new leadership is pushing people out under the umbrella of a new culture and these employees no longer fit. I am always disappointed in leaders who are abrupt liquidators of talent and have not tried to motivate and influence an organization to change. The reason it does not happen is more about the leadership than it is about the people. The opportunity to grow will be missed without a strong level of organizational commitment that pushes itself continuously to improve what it offers to consumers. The S Factor in retail is an operational issue that requires leadership from the CEO to ensure that the longevity of the brand is being managed.

Any retailer will tell you that when all of the drivers in the S Factor are missing, those are the stores that most field managers want to avoid on the way home on a Friday night. To prevent that Friday afternoon terror, they need to rebuild their stores, regions and markets to reflect the true essence of the brand's equity.

Executive Notes: Service is not about Price!

Too often organizations fail at understanding the relationship between service and retention and it is usually confused by developing pricing strategies, simply that has never worked. That is why retailers continuously experience their customers shifting and trialing other retailers, they are looking for the S Factor where it makes sense.

- Your objective is to internally align the organization on what service means and how it must be delivered.
- Don't allow your organization to launch sales strategies without service as the driving component.
- Incorporate your own version of the S Factor.
- Make the aspects of service tangible and measurable and track improvements.
- Consider how to engage the entire organization down the same path.
- This is a leadership initiative with an unusually strong focus to deliver the strategy.
- You will not achieve your sales objectives without an S Factor in your business.

Priority IV: Lead Responsibly - Influence and Direction

YOUR FOURTH PRIORITY IS TO ensure that customers, employees, and stakeholders all benefit from the organization you built.

You cannot dismiss the importance of corporate governance either in a privately – or publicly-operated company. Boards of directors have a unique responsibility of stewardship over the success of publicly-traded retailers. Every time I read about another failing retail brand I wonder, when did the board realize that something was wrong and why didn't they act faster? Do we as leaders understand how important corporate social responsibility is?

Chapter 17: Beyond the Financials

PRINCIPLE 17: YOU CAN'T EXIST in retail without the right financial culture.

You learn very early in the retail industry that you can only run with negative sales and profit numbers for so long before the banks and shareholders will point out that you are no longer a credit-worthy or viably profitable company. Suppliers cut you off, payrolls are missed, rents are late, and eventually businesses fail. This dark reality is the outcome for weaker chains and independent retail operators around the world.

The pressure on retailers to deliver short-term results increases when they begin to lose their appeal with consumers and slip from relevance. Growth is no longer as easy as it once was when they first launched their brand. The proposition to run a business in this manner and environment loses its appeal with many executives realizing that they are now in a trap to drive profit growth and the matter of growing share doesn't seem as important. Unfortunately, when in this type of situation, it becomes difficult to focus on strategies that can reenergize an organization and its results.

The fourth priority in this book is to indicate the importance of running a responsible retail company. And no retailer would be responsible if it didn't have the right level of financial analysis and reviews in place. However, these practices are sometimes inadequate at identifying and addressing the real risks and opportunities. To accomplish this objective, a retail organization needs to ensure that its business review practices allow for open dialogue on business improvement opportunities, and it should avoid the following common mistakes.

Opportunity #1: Monday Morning Sales Reviews

Week-ending business summaries are ineffective when all they accomplish is a rehash the previous week's sales results. The boring and dreaded Monday meetings plague every industry. Yet the process doesn't have to be so negative or draining. These meetings can be made more productive when you trace the previous week's results back to marketing campaigns, sales promotions, staff incentives, or product initiatives that are counted on to deliver the current quarters financial objectives. These meetings should be focused on what else can be done to improve performance. The previous week's sales results shouldn't take more than five minutes to review, and the rest of the discussion should be based on where and how to address weak areas in the business.

Opportunity #2: Structured Field Reporting

The best-run retail organizations have structured retail reporting systems in place that create consistency in the field and throughout the retail organization. The best-in-class weekly business reporting focuses on key measures that are important to the organization achieving its overall financial and customer-related objectives. Good leaders will also take their team through a constructive dialogue to understand whether the stores (regions or markets) that are underperforming are either not responding to strategy or lack execution. While the majority of organizations follow a similar process, they lack the specificity of which business results to focus on and the healthy nature of constructive dialogue to uncover and improve upon risks and opportunities. The reason for this is a lack of systems to follow up and track the progress of these meetings and their findings. Marketers and financial analysts should be able to pull this weekly feedback from markets to the detail that the front line operators understand it.

Opportunity #3: Functional Direction

I have found that general management meetings, whether weekly business reviews or monthly financial analyses, are not always effective at building consensus and direction. The best opportunity is to have functional leaders reiterate how their team is performing against agreed upon objectives and their contribution to financial targets. Again, ensure meetings include a constructive process that allows key leaders and their direct reports to gain insight into the business and further enhance their abilities to improve performance within their function and that of the broader organization. If a retailer is like our hypothetical scenario in Chapter 5, functions need more than a boost in the arm, they require direction and assurances that their efforts are in the right direction.

Opportunity # 4: Communication

What's usually missing in communication is the quality and consistency of the message. Too often the method of how messages are relayed is usually the problem. It is the CEO's responsibility to ensure that direction and recent results are properly conveyed to the organization. Missing this opportunity to create consistency and focus will be overridden by hearsay and disjointed opinions delivered by less informed managers. Management must provide teams with a thorough understanding of what the numbers mean beyond the impact on the Profit and Loss Statement. Management should be able to state specifically the steps that functional and operational teams need to make to improve performance. Retail leaders that can appreciate the value in creating a culture where it is healthy to review results in a constructive manner and openly challenge functions, people and resources without demeaning them will achieve greater clarity and internal competitiveness to deliver the right results. Some leaders who do the opposite create fear and protectionist behaviours that eventually will hurt the organization.

Nothing can replace sound finance and accounting functions and I have been a part of two such organizations with that level of discipline in my career. However, not every organization is as focused and as disciplined at delivering a level of analysis and forensic like dissections of their business to understand cause and effect. Beyond the numbers exists something more and that is the human interaction and skill of listening to the operators and their concerns about the performance of the business. If your functional teams are not able to collect the right level of information from your field operations, the likelihood is that someone is guessing about the true nature of the issues or what the leadership team wants to hear. In either situation it is not going to help your organization grow.

If you want better results look and listen to the facts about the implementation and execution of your strategies. If sales are not being achieved it is either a lack of execution or the wrong strategy and no leader wants to hear about either especially in an industry where consumers judge their every experience on your ability to execute. The only way to guarantee strong execution is to operate a retail organization that is focused on staying relevant and that task as I said earlier belongs to senior management and the board of directors.

Executive Notes: The Numbers are Important

- Listen carefully to the feedback on the financial results do the numbers match the operational execution?
- Place your emphasis on execution are we delivering what we said we would?
- Create a dash board that tells you about product, conversion, traffic, labour hours versus traffic, sales per hour, transactions per hour, transactions per productive hour. Was your brand ready to deliver the service experience when the customers were there?
- Have specific meeting practices on Mondays that ensure effective communication.
- Drill down into the details, for example: knowing how many stores made the forecast and how many didn't may not be exciting to some, but it is one of the most important exercises in retail.
- Field business reporting and the way it is structured needs to have an end goal in mind with a great deal of follow up at next week's meeting.
- Get your functional teams comfortable with open communication – it's about improving the overall business results.
- Have your CFO involved in weekly operational updates with a specific role. Sometimes organizations that are large miss this opportunity.
- Invite field managers to sit in on organizational business updates. Ask them lots of questions!
- The closer the CEO and CFO get to the business the more effective they can make the meetings and focus on performance improvements.

Chapter 18: Governance and Organizational Responsibility

PRINCIPLE 18: CORPORATE SOCIAL RESPONSIBILITY is not going away; it is going to transfer into other shapes and forms of focus that society sees as important. It will be best that your organization identifies them first.

I am intrigued by corporate social responsibility (CSR) as a subject, especially as it relates to the responsibilities bestowed on CEOs and boards of directors. Countless companies get it and have embraced CSR as the right thing to do. Companies constantly face risks; it is the nature of being in business, and without some risk there is no reward. The responsibility to manage risks rests with management and the boards that they report to (if there is one), along with developing enterprise risk management (ERM) evaluations and audits. Conducting these internal audits provides an organization with the knowledge of potential issues and the inherent risks that can be harmful to the company's future and the potential fallout it poses to society.

Unfortunately, risks and mismanagement continue to occur in all types of organizations. Companies either fail to continue as viable businesses or cause harm as result of their inactions. I don't believe that everything is preventable. However, we can make ourselves more aware of the potential risks and design plans to eliminate or manage them. Yet companies will continue to fail and make mistakes. These organizations are led by very well-educated and experienced business people, so what happens to their duty to act? When did they know that something was going wrong? And if they knew, why didn't they act faster? Often these are unanswered questions. How does it relate to retail?

Retailers' Social Responsibility

A major social responsibility of retailers is to ensure that they deal fairly with consumers and safeguard them from harmful or dangerous products, in addition to protecting consumers from inappropriate and misguided pricing practices. Your employees also want to ensure that they work for a reputable company that provides them with fair and equitable work practices. Since many of these retailers are either publicly-traded corporations or are owned by private equity firms, they have a reputation to protect.

Corporate social responsibility goes beyond 'going green,' and sustainability has many measures beyond the environment – not that they are unimportant. We live in an age where the next generation of consumers will have a greater reverence for brands that respect society, cultural differences, and the environment, and that shun manufacturing in countries with questionable labour and political practices. In exchange for all of this, consumers will be willing to pay a premium for doing business with a socially responsible company.

Businesses that embrace CSR show through their actions that they value their people, communities, shareholders, and business partners. The benefits of CSR to retailers are many, from enhanced reputation and loyal consumers to a more committed workforce. Through CSR, retailers can enhance recruitment and retention rates as well as strengthen their bottom line. In fact, there is growing evidence that companies with CSR strategies outperform their counterparts.

The issue that many retailers face with CSR is that it will create a line on the profit and loss statement. Not unlike other branding efforts, it is difficult to equate the cost of CSR initiatives and their impact on performance immediately. However, the purpose of CSR is not to turn a profit from it, but to demonstrate that your brand understands its relationship to society: being a trusted employer, providing ethical goods, and setting an example for suppliers that want to conduct business with you. At the end of the day it is difficult to place financial cost on CSR, although the long-term effects on profitability will come about out of greater customer loyalty.

CSR is going to become a reputational measure for organizations in the future. Imagine a society turning against a retailer for layoffs, closing of stores and plants, hiring underage workers at a manufacturing centre overseas, using harmful material, selling defective products, and not being able to sustain a viable business. It may sound very out of control, however that is what the social media and networks around the world have the power to deliver. A retailer that values its reputation has no choice but to carefully look at CSR as a strategy.

Retailers that fail to incorporate CSR into their strategies at this transformative time in their industry do so at their peril. However, a strong CSR strategy goes beyond corporate governance. It crosses over into managing different cultures, opening into new markets and appreciating the differences in diversity. It is extremely important that you pay attention to your activities when you cross borders, particularly in countries where child labour and work conditions are an ongoing issue. Retailers need to see this as a competitive advantage and set the stage for the world to recognize that they have a great deal of respect for behaving and conducting their activities in an appropriate manner.

Through a commitment to CSR you will be able to gain long-term relevance with consumers and existing customers. I also believe that over time the gap between mass retailers that practice CSR will receive the same benefits and respect that luxury brands are able to command. The performance of these retailers will come through their day to day activities with their employees, and if they can make believers out of them they in turn will take care of the customer who will also believe it.

Executive Notes: CSR Needs to Move From Paper to Action

As an advocate of strong Board performance and effective Corporate Social Responsibility I believe that both can no longer ignore one another or their own duties to the organization.

- Begin with the leaders of the organization. A demonstrated commitment to internal programs that create a stronger culture and focus on what's meaningful to the organization is a great start.
- Take business partners along into this transformation. Suppliers need to respect your quest to run a complete sustainable business.
- Remember that your employees are your greatest asset. As your internal partners, when they understand why something is important, an organization can have no greater commitment.
- Recognize CSR as a competitive advantage within your organization and evolve its importance with your customers. Find ways to impress upon your customers that they too have a duty.
- Ensure corporate boards also embrace CSR and ask the challenging questions of management:
    - Where are our opportunities?
    - What risks do we face that could affect our reputation?
    - How much further ahead are our competitors?
    - Will our activities with CSR be believable by our customers and suppliers?
    - Who should lead it internally? How do we lead from our current position?

It may difficult for many retailers to accept that this is the right game-changing idea to drive growth. Yet consider this: society's tolerance of less responsible organizations that harm the environment, abuse employees, sell less reliable products, and take advantage of situations for profit without weighing out the consequences do themselves and their shareholders harm.

Chapter 19: Where Was the Board?

PRINCIPLE 19: DEFINE THE BOARD'S role and establish how can it be more effective in building a great retail brand.

Many corporate boards are extremely well run and have the wherewithal to ask all the right questions and ensure that management is heading in the right direction. Alternatively, in some boards it doesn't seem like anyone was watching the fallout as it occurred. Performance of a corporate board governing a retail company requires more attention to strategic details than one might think.

The Board's Role

Throughout this book I have been pointing out the importance of remaining relevant in a highly evolving and competitive market. And yet, as much as we would expect an involved board of directors, the media alerts us to situations where an organization has once again missed sales for three quarters in a row, misinterpreted the market conditions, pursued the wrong strategies, or committed some environmental error. Again and again we should ask, how is it the board didn't act on these issues? What questions were asked of the CEO? Did the board fail to get the right information or fail to act on it? Although this is part of the problem, it is also my view that boards are not aware of how volatile the retail market has become. The idea that things may settle down and or rebound in the next quarter is no longer the norm.

Retail corporate boards need to be as active as the market is fluid. The chair, CEO and board members need to have a higher level of communication and question the current conditions and judgment behind decisions. In essence, a board needs to be far more active with respect to strategy, including its formulation, implementation, and execution. This is where I believe the recent failures of retail companies lies: the board is too far removed from strategy, and as a result many opportunities are missed to correct the course of action or pursue the next generation of growth.

When retail companies conduct searches for new CEOs, it is not a leader with past board experience that is mandatory as much as a retail executive with general management experience who knows how to define the right strategies and move the retail brand to its next phase of growth or corrective course. Publicly-traded retail organizations are always looking for the white knight who can save the company. We all know that is rare, and someone's success in one company is not always transferable or repeatable somewhere else.

The demise of book, video, and music stores as a segment in the retail industry is an ongoing debate, in the opinion of many, has been at the hands of Amazon. Why did this happen? Usually because someone was not asking the right questions about strategy and the current situation. Amazon was fast at introducing breakaway strategies and products. Simply, these offline retailers who knew where the opportunities to further expand their businesses existed but did not pursue them. This is especially true in segments of the retail market where competition can be intense and the unpredictable forces of disruptive business models increase in their presence and activities. No one believed that online retailing would become a major threat, and everyone likely agreed to deal with it later. Yet this is not only about online threats, it is new country entrants that are able to change the consumers thinking on how to buy specialty products and department store chains that can gain instant market share because of their brands success elsewhere. All of this is the responsibility of management to bring it to the attention of their board and yet it does not happen as quickly as it should or there was not enough information to highlight the risks.

What is the Role of the Board?

In all practical terms, boards are temporary and casual stewards of a business. They provide guidance and ensure that management makes good on their commitment to deliver a plan. Nothing states that a board has to be made up of a certain set of skilled experts although it is presumed. It is important to have a diverse board one that can impact on the business. However, what is paramount it must be a board that is involved.

The role of the board of directors is to ensure the successful implementation and execution of strategy by management. In addition to this their role is to deliver financial results for the shareholders and to see it that the financial reporting and risks of the organization are properly documented and audited for presentation to shareholders. When an audit committee is apprised of risks, they need to report them and risks are not limited to cost management or liabilities related to lawsuits, they include (should include) competitive risks.

Competitive risks are something that falls under the category of Enterprise Risk Management (ERM). Therefore, if we were able to look into the minutes of these defunct video, book, and music store chains was the risk of online retailers highlighted and did the management and board of each of these organizations address the issue with a workable plan or was it dismissed? That would be for academics to dig into. My argument is that they likely didn't expect it to be as important a threat. Therefore, the opportunity to remain relevant by pursuing a tangible strategic response was not undertaken fast enough. I underline the word fast because we should ask when was the board made aware. And did management even know they were losing share so quickly?

The board has a duty to care about the wellbeing of the corporation and to do that effectively they need to be aware of the issues internally and externally faced by the business. That requires a time commitment to understand the financials, be very aware of the corporate strategies and be prepared to ask the tough questions others may not be able to ask.

Questions for the Chief Executive Officer

In most case studies conducted on the failure of companies and that covers all industries, the underlying issue has been the board did not probe enough to determine the strength and effectiveness of the company's strategies.

Directors in companies need to ask the tough questions at quarterly meetings and it's not enough to simply overview the financials. The board must correlate the effectiveness of strategies versus the financial results being achieved. And it doesn't matter if the results were exceeding expectations.

- Are the current strategies on track?
- What are the potential risks to our strategic plans?
- How are you tracking those risks and are appropriate responses ready to be executed?
- Which of our strategies are effectively delivering our financial results?
- Can you identify for the board which strategies are not delivering results and what action steps are being taken to resolve them?
- Are there internal issues that might get in the way of delivering plan?
- Is our plan still valid given the current market situations?

These questions and others like them, get to the core of what you need to know beyond the quarterly package you receive from management. Asking the right questions also opens the door for management to be more candid and feel that the board is a partner.

Accelerating Board Performance

The makeup of retail boards is something that needs to also be considered as a means to improve performance. Without understanding the needs of each business, it will be difficult to state with clarity what needs to change within a specific type of retail brand and its board. However, I would ensure that the competencies of the board include e-commerce experience, strategy experts, and a healthy background in industries where change and the need to continually reinvent the business are paramount to success. No board is infallible, yet the need of a board to demonstrate a 'duty to care' is something that is non-negotiable. Many CEO's argue that they want their boards to be more engaged in a supporting role that allows for greater exchange of ideas and support.

A board's performance is a delicate matter that is filled with personal and business risks about managing strategy and the priorities of the corporation. Your role on a board is that of a directing mind that comes with fiduciary duty. Your past business experience is needed to help direct the course of the organization.

Initially there are six key aspects to a higher performance board as it relates to a director's role in any type of organization:

Knowledge and Awareness – It is important that you thoroughly understand the complexities of the business you are acting as board member for. Past annual reports, strategic reviews, and audit reports are all available to understand the past and current state of the business. In addition, a tour of all business aspects is a very good initiation.

Active: Be Inquisitive and Engaged – As a board member, you must ask a lot of questions and not be afraid to engage even the group thinking of the board. Often I am told that it is not the board's responsibility to be operational. While I agree, when performance of management and the results are poor, following that protocol will not help either.

Fiduciary Duty – You are responsible for the best interests of the organization. That means that as a steward, you are accountable for ensuring that the organization is heading in the right direction with all the objectives you have charged the CEO to deliver.

Risk Management – All businesses face risks. Some of them turn into opportunities, while in extreme cases others can cause disasters. Without proper enterprise risk management (ERM) and effective ranking of these risks in terms of their likelihood of occurring, boards can be liable for not doing their part to mitigate the organization's exposure. This is especially true if you were aware of the risks and the potential harm to the business and society and did not act on it.

Performance Evaluations – Every board must know its mission and strategic plan that drives it, followed by objectives, plans, and tactics. While it all sounds simple, why do so many companies continue to fail, misrepresent their financials, or allow officers of the company to continue in their role with a downward impact on financials, share price, market share and customer satisfaction? Organizations with strong corporate governance use performance evaluations to manage their own performance. The use of board evaluations as an assessment tool for board member performance is only effective when it goes beyond just a process. When the chair and the board of governance committee can improve the performance of a board member, then it is an effective tool.

Corporate Governance – To achieve a higher level of performance, a board must set clear governance practices. This will define the level of performance expected from its board members. In addition, a recruitment matrix can evolve from these practices that better defines the competencies and capabilities a selection committee needs to fill its future bench for management and the board itself. How does this all relate to the retail industry? It is exactly the same as it would be for other industries: it comes down to CSR. No one wants a board that is not actively engaged in the successful performance and reputation of their company.

Retail organizations that are publicly traded need to evaluate the relevance of their board members versus the needs of the business and that includes changes in the economy, political events, competitive threats, and international expansion. Management must keep the board apprised and the board must remind management where their reporting relationship is with the combined accountability to keep the company relevant and profitable. The board and its members need to be equally comfortable with challenging one another and the manner with which they evaluate the business collectively and independently.

Executive Notes: Corporate Governance keeping the House in Order

Directors have a difficult task as part-time stewards for a business, they need to rely on the management team bestowed with operational duties to deliver on the objectives and strategies agreed on.

- Boards need to strike a balance for its members between past board experience and relevant business experience.
- The audit committee needs to ensure that not only the numbers are accurately reported but that the implementation and execution of the strategies are a reflection of those results.
- The boards of retail brands need to appreciate that they need to be much more inquisitive in this business as the level of volatility is far greater.
- There is always the risk that boards can be too engrained in process only and not focus enough on execution of their duties.
- Strategy and financial performance of the business should be the board's main priorities.
- Cultural management is also an important priority within strategic management.

Chapter 20: The Competitive Advantage of Employee Engagement

Principle 20: If people are really your most important asset, what have you done lately to convince them of that?

At a time when the world remains uncertain about its prospects, competition for talent and customers will become more aggressive. Companies in all industries that create a strong culture of employee engagement will benefit from its effectiveness. Those that have an internal employee engagement strategy also have a competitive advantage that is not easy to dismiss.

The Importance of Employee Engagement

Business recognizes that employee retention is of critical importance. With the loss of talent, their capabilities also exit, potentially bringing about irreversible negative results including the cost associated with lost customers. Equally significant is the opportunity to attract new employees and customers, which should be at the forefront of every CEO's agenda. If every CEO could deliver organizational employee engagement, it would mean the difference between mediocrity and outstanding performance. Every organization should be striving to score high on creating a culture of high productivity, strategic innovation and customer satisfaction, ending with improved sales and profits.

Organizations that are unable to achieve strong employee engagement will continue to meet with high turnover; poor performance, or employees who have lost confidence in management and are fearful of excessive change, seeking a third party to represent them or leaving altogether. It is easy to see what's missing in a corporate culture like this one and the damage that it can cause in market performance.

How to Improve Employee Engagement

Employee engagement is not something that you can simply command to start on its own, nor is it part of your leadership style and charisma, because that is not always enduring. Without a comprehensive strategic plan, change management of this nature is something that should not be entrusted to your direct reports only. It will not be delivered by sheer will or in a separate meeting. It is a culture that must be built from the inside out, and it begins with a total commitment to your corporate values, how you define leadership, and ensuring you practise what you preach.

I have found through experience that when employees begin to focus on their income as a measure of their contribution, the company is failing to challenge these employees with the right work and sense of organizational and individual purpose. The reasons employees joined your company include your company's mission, vision and values, commitment to technology, development of people, quality manufacturing, and green initiatives, to name a few. Organizations need something that will connect with their employees' sense of purpose.

No change management program is easy to achieve. Changes initiated without well thought out plans tend to disappear early. It is simply about creating a culture that has a strong sense of employee engagement. Of course, just like the products and services your company sells, it is difficult to be all things to all people.

Since no single strategy suits all, a process of corporate discovery is a beginning.

Define what is significant externally and internally. Why does your company exist? How do you create value in the lives of your customers? What will inspire your employees to come in every morning, excited to return to work? The leadership of the organization needs to demonstrate a commitment that is powerful enough to create change.

Take every opportunity to raise the profile of your community activities for your employees, customers, and suppliers. Everyone wants to know where and how their company is contributing toward that powerful cause. Be careful not to exploit these activities with your need to drive sales and profits. Keep these activities separate from your business operations, making them part of your day-to-day culture.

Develop activities that will involve everyone during the course of the year. This is an opportunity to demonstrate your commitment to your employees and stakeholders. Make them events that everyone looks forward to for solidifying your organization's goodwill.

Make employee engagement programs part of your annual objectives. Focus on creating a higher level of ownership within the company at all levels. Introduce it in your performance evaluations as a measure for reinforcing the values and their importance to the long-term health of the company.

Solidify your focus on building an engaged company by promoting and encouraging internal volunteerism. It must always begin with a senior leadership team that believes and visibly participates in the activities.

Create an open forum for your employees to talk about your employee engagement initiatives. What has their personal experience with helping others or volunteering meant to them? Along the way, recognize and reward employees and stakeholders for the contributions to corporate social responsibility (CSR).

These activities do not have to cost a great deal of money; in fact, when the initiatives can save money and create goodwill, the return will be greater. Cultural change takes time. It is not something that will emerge on its own, but rather requires leadership, passion, and commitment. To avoid all the pitfalls of failing organizations, consider how a change in a culture that promotes employee involvement can change the course of your company and potential.

Executive Notes: Do you recognize that people are your greatest asset?

Consider this, you run a retail organization and the sales and management teams operating your stores have absolute authority over the head count you have in your home office to support your stores. The retail team can reduce hours and replace the leaders within each function as business results dictate. If that makes you uncomfortable now you know why store results are not consistent.

- Employee engagement weakens with decisions that are counter-intuitive to your words and actions.
- Not everyone will respond to your charitable intentions. Find common ground.
- Employee engagement does not mean a bigger budget. It does, however, mean doing a better job communicating what you do for your people.
- Be open to feedback about your practices.
- Focus on every generation of workers coming into the workplace; your efforts cannot be only about serving one demographic.
- Do your succession planning practices show you as an employer of equal opportunity or one that is closed to the opinions of a few?
- Get yourself and your leadership team out into the stores clear your agenda for a couple of days a month including travel.

Chapter 21: Personal Social Responsibility – Cultural Divides

PRINCIPLE 21: PERSONAL SOCIAL RESPONSIBILITY is about the reputation of the individual.

While we understand CSR corporate social responsibility, we also need to understand PSR, personal social responsibility and what it means within the context of running a responsible company. In some form of this concept, human resources, the CEO and the board have a responsibility to set the proper expectations beyond performance and personal behaviour.

Personal social responsibility is a leadership quality that in my opinion has been missed over the last twenty years; we have placed greater value on personal style, motivation, communication, and inspiration as some of the key leadership traits. However today while these and other traits remain important we need to add PSR to the equation. I believe that as leaders we have a responsibility to society when we assume the roles in organizational, political, or theological offices. And yes, that social responsibility also reaches the individuals within these institutions, whether they are within a functional role, in retail operations, or sitting on a board of directors. PSR needs to be a measure of confidence that management has in the people they place in key roles, those who must demonstrate the values of the organization and be good spokespeople for the retail organization. Too often internal politics destroy the trust that good PSR practices can deliver and obstruct the stage for important developmental and behavioural changes within the organization.

In a world where information, opinions, and news reaches the masses quickly, the damage that a leader with a poor PSR rating can have on a business is dramatic and ultimately a negative impact on the brand's stock price, equity with consumers, and trust with their employees. We have already seen how fast consumers can react to changes in their preference to utilize discounts and how shareholders will dump a stock with the board's, choice over a CEO or a board's, decision not to act on poor performance.

Personal social responsibility is not something that public relations firms or psychological assessments can resolve with personal coaches. The main issues are the behaviours of leaders who are in roles of authority and believe that they are untouchable given their position taking risks and displaying conduct that offends customers, employees, shareholders, and business partners. More specifically, this can take the form of allowing or being involved in improper personal relationships, or even abuse of employees, company assets, authority, and information. Taking risks that cause harm to reputation and people who work for the company or society in general (we've seen this recently in oil companies). At one time ethics and integrity were widely used as words to describe what companies were looking for in their leadership teams. I do not believe that we have gone far enough. PSR should include knowing when your decisions, actions, and behaviours risk hurting other people and organizations. That also places emphasis on leading responsibly and when you fail to do so you fail many constituents. And while we could argue that CSR and PSR may mean the same thing with respect to management and a board of directors, they do not. PSR defines the character of the individual leader, the principles they use to get results and the effect it has on the organization. You cannot have a board member sit idle and not act on an issue that would negatively impact the image of a company – that would be poor PSR on their part. On the other hand when one set of standards that are applied broadly throughout an organization no leader should be allowed to abuse those standards in any form of poor conduct. Doing so does not demonstrate an organization with the leadership maturity of PSR and reduces the value of their CSR practices.

Imagine a business leader from the UK asking an employee in France to do something about the unfair labour laws and severance practices in the employee's home country. Ridiculous, you might say? It happens. Retail corporations, whether in their own home country or another country, derail all the goodwill they have developed when such incidents occur. While the above example may be extreme, it is impossible for employees to believe that you respect their culture and them, therefore all your best practices are for naught. For an individual to be socially responsible they need to respect society as a whole and understand that their opinions can cause offense and damage to a business.

PSR behaviours are a measure of acts that create perceptions which affect a leader's reputation even if they are not the one who creates the incident. The challenge is that beyond your mission, vision and values, you need to make believers of your constituents – employees, customers and stakeholders – that you are a committed retailer and believe in PSR. Nothing can shatter the good intentions of a new or existing brand's sound business model and excellent CSR practices than lost trust caused by the poor PSR qualities of others.

Human Resources and Culture

Labour laws, cultural beliefs about hierarchy, and the influence of human resources over management are often issues as companies begin to expand across the globe. As retailers cross borders they must have an international view of PSR and the most rational reason for it is that in some countries words such as ethics, morality, and integrity do not translate the same and often fall short of clarifying the expectations for an executive to lead themselves and others by.

The biggest mistake companies make is assuming that their corporate ideology is easily transferable to the various countries where they want to conduct business. That's when they begin to get into a lot of problems, such as:

1. Assuming that all employees have the same needs and wants
2. Selling products that do not fit the local culture
3. Trying to transfer corporate cultures and beliefs
4. Assuming that leadership means the same thing here as it does back home
5. Deciding to run a country business like a regional office

6. Handling the marketing and human resources management from their home office

7. Not providing international job postings to international employees

Inevitably, companies that practise in this manner run into three major business issues. The first is that they fail to maximize their full business potential. Secondly, over time they alienate local employees by their foreign cultural beliefs and best practices. And third, when a foreign manager is placed into the leadership position that has little or no international business experience, it opens the door to cultural risks.

Organizations with global expansion plans and a keen interest in Asia, South America, or South Africa must have strong and culturally respectful leadership. The development and introduction of PSR will make it easier to engage your new employees and customers is an important first step. As mentioned earlier, the right CSR strategies make advocates of your employees, customers, and stakeholders. Countless retailers globally are looking to emerging markets as their next green field for expansion. How they accomplish that goal is related to their ability to manage and lead across cultures and monitoring the PSR of the leaders that they send internationally is just as critical as making the decision to expand internationally.

Executive Notes: Personal Social Responsibility Creates a New Paradigm for Leaders

There was a time where an executive would be given the keys to the corner office and asked to do their best as the new CEO. Those days are over. The role now comes with a higher level of accountability, which has many stakeholders and expectations for leaders to deliver results and protect the brand from any negative publicity, internal and external.

- PSR begins with the individual – they either have the maturity to understand it or they don't.
- Just because a country's population may speak English doesn't mean they're culturally the same as North America.
- Evaluate the PSR qualities of your leaders, do they mirror your CSR strategies.
- Carefully consider the reputation and goodwill you want to start building with employees and new customers.
- Don't dismiss the differences in diversity within countries as just nuances.
- Don't assume that all countries respect your beliefs. Many countries have a "me first" cultural belief, so be clear about the PSR values you want from executives.
- If you have a member on your home team that is working with an international team but is insensitive to cultural differences, remove him or her from that project immediately.
- In international reporting relationships leaders with strong PSR qualities can deal with the candour and differences in opinions from others in different countries.
- Your objective in bridging a cultural divide begins with creating a sustainable business culture. The higher your focus on employee PSR as it relates to your CSR activities, the greater the impact to your long-term growth.

Chapter 22: Last Retailer Standing

At the beginning of the book I talked about Johnny's convenience store and how that type of business failure continues today. It is as if no lessons have been learned. Johnny's business life was much like Hemmingway's path to bankruptcy: "At first gradually and then suddenly."

The intent behind the title of the book is to get your attention that the risk of failure has never been higher. Certainly, there will be more than one survivor in the world of retail. Yet in the next decade, it will be dramatically different marketplace than it is today. And the largest retailers are gearing up now for what will be a very competitive environment.

And as of the writing of this chapter in July 2012, analysts are in shock that the US retail market has declined by 0.5%. Those of us working within this industry are not surprised that the numbers are down. The consumer is as sensitive as a patient who has just had major surgery; any changes in bed position will cause extreme pain. And this economy has created a great deal of pain for many globally, retailers and consumers alike.

The Future of the Retail Industry

Several scenarios are going to play out while we are in this economic slump:

Consolidation – There will be a good deal of opportunity for key retailers with similar competencies to merge. International retailers will likely move on opportunities to improve their global footprint with brands from other countries. All of this will occur while capital is cheap and a few businesses need to be saved from the high cost of their infrastructure.

Fewer Store Counts – I don't believe stores will vanish as some have indicated, although there will be fewer stores and many will downsize to manage their costs. As I mentioned in an earlier chapter, your virtual store will need to be an extension of the total in-store experience or it will be capital ill-spent.

Corporate Social Responsibility – No retailer or businesses in other industries should dismiss the importance of CSR. Think of the Occupy Wall Street Movement which was seen in many countries along with mass protests over austerity measures. I am not convinced that these protests are over. Also, consider the protests in 2012 by students in Quebec over small increases in tuition. These are not singular events in time, they are emotional messages. When companies and institutions fail and the boards or politicians that are their stewards fail to protect the employees, shareholders and citizens, society will no longer take it lightly. All of this is an outcome of the above and the result of almost five difficult financial years and the power of social media. If retailers don't believe they should invest heavily in managing their reputations and market positions, they will face some very hard lessons.

Virtual Stores – Retailers will and should pursue a virtual store environment now. That may be a challenge for some organizations before they can pull the right resources and strategies together to make it happen. A virtual store needs to be more than a web page where you can peruse product or flip product pages and look for the next deal. That isn't good enough. In fact, consumers may make shopping destination choices based on the quality and navigable aspects of your virtual store. Consumers need to be able to try on clothing in their own avatar image, and your virtual service staff should be able to make personal recommendations. Once satisfied that they have made the right choices, they place the order and it is either shipped to their home or they pick it up from one of your locations.

Online Versus Offline Retailing – Online retailers are going to overwhelm the market with different models and easier to understand pricing strategies. While they still have logistics opportunities and costs to overcome, the high cost of operating multiple offline locations will not be a burden. It is likely that you will also continue to see breakaway online models that will challenge the core of what was once thought unavailable or impossible to sell, such as medical devices and medicine. Online will be the number one competitive force undermining many brands. As much as retailers hate being contested about price, it will be the main motivator for those consumers shifting their shopping behaviours. Offline retailers can no longer afford to be concerned about what will happen to the offline stores if their online sales grow and decrease the profitability of some stores. Survival is now the only debate and everyone must actively preserve the future of their business.

Single Store Operators – Independent retailers with the right business model may have the opportunity to be more competitive than ever before. They are no longer that single store on the street just picking up whatever business they can. They have an opportunity to make a significant difference in their future, especially with a strong online strategy and external supply chain relationships. Recently a pawn shop store was closing up after some 40 years of business, the owner blamed numerous online competitors who changed his game. That is the unfortunate part for independent retailers, if you don't see how quickly your business can be affected by change you will be a victim like the pawn shop owner or Johnny, the convenience store owner.

Department Stores – Traditional department stores, not the large discount retailers such as Wal-mart, are in need of major changes, such as determining the right number of stores and creating a resurgence of a magical service experience that was once the norm. Department stores, in a sense, have become the anchor of retail, and I don't mean anchor tenants. Most are slow to move in a new direction and it is as if they are constantly in the milking stage. In other instances, as we have recently witnessed in the US, attempts to move a department store from its discounting practices to everyday pricing is a difficult strategy to succeed with. Department stores need to invest and experiment a little more broadly with fashion and designer departments, while still making those products affordable to the middle class. Consumers want a pleasant, higher level service shopping experience in a department store. Unfortunately, some of the heavy cost cutting has been to the detriment of these giants of retail. In order to have a return to their glamour days, they will need to reinvest and reinvent a little from the past and the future.

This may mean a more high-tech experience in department stores where service will be more difficult to rebuild to its past best days.

Chain Stores – With thousands of chains in the global market, each with 100–1,000 stores, we can only expect that weaker retailers with low relevance and low growth will fail within the next 18 to 24 months. A retail brand and its leadership that has the vision to recognize that they are in an industry with short-term business life cycles will continually look for ways to stay relevant. Many retailers today are also racing to reduce the impact of the many sales events that have been created. The risk is that the consumer has been trained not to trust any price, especially when a retailer that boasts the lowest price is also saying "If you find it elsewhere for less, I will refund you the difference." How can they trust you? I do not believe that many will succeed at changing their discounting practices, quite simply it will only open up to other discount schemes. In the end it still comes down to remaining relevant and retailers that do this effectively will remain viable and attractive to each generation of consumers. CEOs and boards of directors will have to act faster and have greater involvement to protect the future of their companies.

A Final Word on Leadership

So much of what happens to each retailer will be dependent on their choice of CEO and that executive's PSR qualities. I believe that in the next decade, retail is going to need strong leadership with executives who are true generalists, and who also have the skills to craft effective change and inspire an organization to new levels of performance and service. They will need to be great communicators and strategists, engaging ideas from all levels internally and externally. Within all of that, they need to know that their job is to keep the brand relevant for the long-term, and that will mean whatever evolution needs to be embraced. The rise of the generalist in the retail world is about to become even more important than the past. While the specialists have had great success in the past, technology and the consumer has changed all of that.

Perhaps the next question we all want answered is: who will be around 10, 15, or 20 years from now? And how will they accomplish it? That will not be easy to determine. However, I am convinced that retailers who understand the importance of remaining relevant know they must embrace technology, develop strong CSR strategies, and seize the opportunity to continuously reinvent their brand. They must keep in mind that retail will continue to be a transient industry as consumers look for what's new, better, improved, fashionable, and evolutionary from a shopping and service experience. Once again the trick is to know when it is time to begin the next evolution.

When we think about the oldest hotels, restaurants, and retailers still standing, we know that it wasn't luck – it was doing the right things for the long-term with the right culture.

Epilogue

As I write this there is so much in the news about retailers struggling to redefine their identities with consumers, especially in the USA. Followed by another invasion of foreign retailers entering Canada with the likes of Target, J Crew and Nordstrom to name a few and the local retailers bracing for the fallout. Where in India retailers are opposing deregulation allowing foreign retailers to enter their market place and Japanese retailers struggling in China as their relationships are strained.

We have to be self-critical and ask ourselves how did we get here? Could the right leadership have prevented the failure of some of these business models? The answer simply is yes and that would have depended so much on choosing the right strategies. A friend once described a CEO's role to me as being given permission to do whatever you want to do in the school playground with no responsibility to ensure that nothing is destroyed.

In my 20 plus years of retailing, I have found that the best leaders are those who are disciplined, who do not threaten their executives, who do not play politics, and who do not disrespect the recent efforts of former leaders. This is what I have come to understand of Personal Social Responsibility to mean for someone like myself that has had the opportunity to lead domestically in Canada and internationally. Executives with amazing PSR are focused, with the earnest desire to develop a brand with all the corporate resources and personal energy available to them.

In the world of retail, we are told that product and price when right will drive traffic. While it is true that anything can sell for a price, if a retailer wants to be in the game for the long-term, it is not about those two factors alone. The customer's experience cannot be dismissed, and retailers who believe that consumers do not pay attention to the ceiling, floors, or lighting have not visited the restrooms in their department stores. The truth is that it is an issue of capital investment. Ultimately what moment of truth are you positioning for your customers?

Everything about the retail industry is in the details. It doesn't matter what you sell and how you sell it. Customers who are attracted to a certain type of store format will visit that store brand and may purchase from it, provided the entire shopping experience is what they expected from the value proposition. Once again, I bring it back to the importance of retail leaders and their influence on building a strong brand. Sometimes organizations look for a leader with strong financial skills. Others want to bring in a merchandiser. You will find that the best retail executives are those who have honed their skills as executive general managers because they have served in more than one area of the business, and have enough experience to deal with the complexity of leading a retail brand.

It is also my hope that what you have taken away from this book is the importance of your leadership to create the right type of changes and organization. The retail industry does not need caretakers it needs visionaries who understand the brand they are leading and can keep it relevant for the long-term.

Finally, I deliberately chose not to mention more than a few companies in this book because it would be unfair to single out those struggling or wishing to make changes.

Summary of the 21 Principles

Principle 1: Change is imminent.

- You can't escape competitive forces whether from within your own organization or external.
- Pursuing change strategies internally is a health exercise that will reduce the risk of becoming an irrelevant brand.
- When we dismiss changing events as fads or short-term business enterprises, we fail to see the opportunities that they represent.

Principle 2: Protect your organizational culture and build its DNA in a direction that sustains a successful business model for the long-term.

- As a leader, your role is to ensure that the right organizational culture exists.
- Allowing other ideals to infiltrate will gradually erode the discipline and structure you need to drive continuity.
- Your biggest risks are executives who do not understand the importance or agree with the organization's core values and vision.

Principle 3: When change is done properly, it brings to life a culture of innovation and openness that challenges your thinking with an internal eagerness that takes root to continually improve yourself and your results.

- No single leader can influence change alone. It requires an organization to deliver it.

- Getting it right is a task that will take time and detailed activities to achieve.
- Make communication your most important weapon in building and defending your culture.

Principal 4: Build a retail brand with a global perspective.

- Learning from others is an important step in understanding your own strengths and weaknesses.
- Even as an independent retailer, with an attractive online model your customers may be shopping from far and wide.
- Leverage the risks in the market to your advantage.

Principle 5: Always be prepared that your brand will face adversity. The speed with which you correctly or incorrectly address internal and external threats will be the real story.

- Your strategies will only be as good as your insights.
- Avoiding bankruptcy calls for intuition, relevant market insights, a strong plan and even stronger execution.
- Don't dismiss the power of technology and e-commerce. Consumers are adapting while some retailers hope that they don't.

Principle 6: As a CEO, your role is to leave a viable brand behind for the next generation of leaders to grow.

- The average tenure of a CEO today is 2–3 years. Can you make enough changes in this short period of time? You can start the change, however you may never see the outcome. By the time the new CEO enters the arena, the business is starting all over again and the spiral begins once more.
- No team will follow an idealist or someone who doesn't believe in the heritage of the brand.

- CEOs who focus more on building their own team risk losing the support of their organization and competitors can exploit their weaknesses and begin targeting their employees and customers.

Principle 7: Your marketing and strategy teams need to think beyond the reaches of their offline stores. The new economy has added virtual stores to the mix, and retailers need to bring this concept to life. Redefine your business as a disruptive retail brand with a commitment to technology, developing the abilities to deliver the right products and services more efficiently and create new market opportunities.

- Virtual stores that complement the personal interaction received in your offline store must be built with service and speed in mind.
- Everyone has a webpage you can scroll through to look at product. Few have taken it to the level where it interacts with consumers and keeps them engaged from an experience perspective.
- Technological investments will build revenue, and you must find ways to build elements of the experience into your offline stores.

Principal 8: In the old economy, it was about how many points of distribution you had. In the new economy, it's about how you incorporate a virtual store into the mix and keep reaching for more customers.

- Be prepared for your portfolio of stores becoming smaller in number and, more importantly, smaller in size.
- Bring costs down and improve the customer experience.
- Most retailers have cut payroll to the bone. Any further and the checkout staff will be managing the store as well.

Principal 9: What you need to know about conversion is that it is within your control. Whether you want more transactions per customer or more customers converted, all you have to do is train your retail sales team to deliver your processes the right way.

- Retailers are victims of their own choices.

- Less service and fewer selling tools mean fewer sales.
- Not enough training and lack of service standards will cost you more in turnover and lost sales.

Principal 10: When you deliver the right product at the right price in the right environment, it is easier to mitigate the efforts of competitors.

- There is no question that the right product will drive sales.
- Consumers need to know that you have it and that it is available.
- The right product also means that you are setting trends in design and fashion. Do you have the competencies and capabilities internally to deliver that goal?

Principle 11: When it comes to change management, the trick is to know when, how and who should lead it.

- There is little room for error once you begin a change initiative within the organization.
- You must consider the impact on employees, suppliers, and customers. The path you choose may change the paradigm of your business culture so much that many may not agree with your path.
- Improve your communication process if you want buy-in from everyone involved and those affected by change.

Principle 12: Not all leaders are able to manage change. Past success in one organization is not a predictor of future success, nor that it is right for the culture.

- Boards sometimes get buried in the need to fill a position and look for someone who has run a successful brand. Sometimes it's the brand and not the leader.
- The right leaders will embrace the organization with sincerity and honesty, rebuilding it anew from the inside out.

- Look for ways to bring along the organization and profile key employees from different levels of the organization who believe and have demonstrated support for your cause.

Principle 13: Never deny the facts or allow anyone to distort what the facts are telling you.

- The toughest decision leaders can make is to have someone dissect their decisions.
- Conduct an internal stress test on your effectiveness to craft and deliver the right strategies.
- Running a business and believing you know best is a mistake that's meant to protect managerial egos.

Principal 14: Don't believe your own internal press about your position in the marketplace; consumers and competitors may think otherwise.

- Many organizations that have had past success sometimes go through phases of myopia. The first sign is belief that they are unbeatable.
- The executive who still believes in a past promotional event or strategy will wear it down until it has no more life. Window dressing it with a new message doesn't change the declining traffic and customer erosion.
- Market-driven organizations do not allow internal rhetoric to get in the way of continuously rebuilding their brand.

Principle 15: Stay relevant and stay in the game.

- Don't overlook how you can stay competitive in an unforgiving climate with satisfied and dissatisfied consumers sharing their thoughts faster than ever before. Monitor competitors who can make things happen faster with greater efficiency and a better experience.

- Your objective is always to ensure you are relevant. Sometimes this involves the smallest and least expensive changes.

- A retail brand must be an extension of the values and vision of the people who work in the organization. If there is no alignment, then it is a question of poor leadership or poor communication (likely one and the same).

Principle 16: When it comes to growing sales, there is a formula to success. However, the investment in time and resources must be consistent with the desire to grow sales, otherwise there are only limited results and missed opportunities.

- Retailers have decreased service to save costs. In return they get fewer transactions and a higher average sale through price increases. Now they are faced with a consumer that does more research and is unwilling to pay a higher price. If the level of service is the same online, why pay offline prices?

- To have a service-oriented culture you need to have training, backed by standards of performance and the means to measure and expect improvement in overall sales performance.

- Your objective with a service strategy is to sell to more customers and sell more to those same customers.

Principle 17: You can't exist in retail without the right financial culture.

- Spend more time educating the organization about what the results mean and what needs to be done versus allowing field teams to send the wrong message.

- With today's technology, CEOs can no longer expect others to communicate the message.

- The right culture will allow for healthly dialogue between functions to improve results and assist one another to grow the business. There is no room for turf protecting leaders.

Principle 18: Corporate social responsibility is not going away; it is going to transfer into other shapes and forms of focus as society makes them important. It will be best that you identify them first.

- Listen to the outside world and build CSR strategies that are relevant to your business.
- Don't go overboard with idealism. Stay focused on what's important to the values of the organization.
- At the same time, don't be caught off-guard by CSR. Pay attention to your own enterprise risk management evaluations and ensure you don't miss something important.

Principle 19: Know the board's role and how it can be more effective in building a great retail brand.

- A board of directors needs to work with its appointed management team to ensure that members have the skills, resources and focus to deliver a financially viable business for the long-term.
- Boards must check in during all meetings to ensure that the strategies are not being undermined by short-term results.
- Boards must act quicker when results are not being delivered. A drop of 20–30% in sales and profits must be cause for monthly meetings rather than waiting for the next quarter.

Principle 20: If people are really your most important asset, what have you done lately to convince them of that?

- Developing a culture where people feel valued for their contributions will fuel loyalty.
- Rewards for exemplary customer service and sales performance need to be acknowledged, otherwise frontline employees will feel disconnected and unimportant.
- Proper succession planning at all levels provides a sense of opportunity that is available for the right people. However, if you

are unwilling or unable to invest in training and development programs, don't proceed with succession planning efforts because they will not yield you the results that you want.

Principle 21: Personal social responsibility is about the reputation of the individual.

- As retail businesses expand internationally with either offline or online strategies, they need leadership with mature PSR qualities.
- Do not allow leaders with poor PSR qualities to advance in your organization, any of the associated risks will undermine the fabric and trust within your organization.
- PSR should be a part of performance reviews, personal developmental plans and company culture.